Our
Old
House

Our
New
Home

A Practical Real Estate Purchasing Guide

for Active Adults Planning for

Retirement

Our Old House
— Our New Home

**A Practical Real Estate Purchasing Guide for Active
Adults Planning for Retirement**

Copyright 1998 Jared March
Licensed Real Estate Broker and
Senior Housing Marketing Specialist

 Jared March Publishing Group
714 West Bay Avenue
Barnegat, NJ 08005
609 660 2200

ISBN Number 0-931673-11-9
Library of Congress Catalog Card Number
98-092058
Printed in the USA Morris Publishing, Kearney NE
First Edition

Reverse Living

(author unknown)

Life is tough. It takes up a lot of your time— including your weekends. And what do you get at the end of it? — Death — a great reward.

I think that the life cycle is all backwards.

You should die first, and get it out of the way. Then you should live twenty years in an old-age home. They would kick you out when you were too young to stay there. Upon leaving, you'd receive a gold watch and head out to work. You'd work forty years or so until you were young enough to enjoy your retirement.

You'd go to college and experiment with drugs and alcohol and upon graduation you'd head off for high school. After high school you'd attend grade school and then become a little kid again. You'd play, have no responsibilities, and turn into a little baby. You'd be born of a loving Mom then go back into the womb. You'd spend your last nine months floating in water — and finish off as a proud gleam in your father's eye.

IT'S TIME TO PUT THESE AWAY

Foreword

As we get older, the world has a tendency to assume that we are able to weed through all presented information, filter out unimportant facts, and arrive at sound and prudent decisions based upon the remaining data.

For the most part, this is true. But, while the intellegence of senior Americans has lead us into the greatest period of wealth ever imagined, reality has shown us that even the most savvy business person can make poor decisions if ill-advised or under-prepared. This is especially true when the subject matter is unfamiliar or when it is only encountered once or twice during a lifetime.

Buying or selling a home is one of those subjects. Our first purchase, usually when we are just married or having our first baby, is uncomplicated because we rely on the advice of parents and older siblings. We also believe that our inexperienced luck will carry us through to a proper decision. We are for the most part — fearless.

Much later now, retired and with the kids grown and gone, we again enter the real estate environment and seek out that perfect place where we can spend our golden years enjoying favorite activities with new friends of the same age.

But this time shouldn't we be smarter? Shouldn't we make a plan to follow? And shouldn't we make sure that this purchase will have a better than average chance of success so we won't *regret that we didn't buy a different type of residence or home in a different community.*

The real estate purchasing guide that follows is presented to assist the Senior Buyer who is beginning the search for a retirement residence. To date, no one has taken the time to consolidate the important options available nor outlined the personal analysis procedures necessary to make the decision clearer and more reliable.

This book has been written with the practical input of thousands of active adult buyers. Because of the broadness of the information base, you will now be equipped with new and useful information that will help you make the best purchase decision possible.

Yes, Seniors are smart. And yes, they are supposed to know almost everything. But learning never stops. And your last largest purchase of a retirement home will be made simpler if you utilize the principles and selection processes set forth in this book.

— Jared March

TABLE OF CONTENTS

Introduction   9

Part I — Preparing for the Purchase

Chapter One	We Think It's Time To Leave	13
Chapter Two	A Plan for Researching the Move	17
Chapter Three	Setting the Timetable of Events	33
Chapter Four	Asking (Telling) the Kids	41
Chapter Five	Real Estate Community Choices	45

- *Existing Retirement Communities*   47
- *Active Adult Communities*   48
- *All-Age Communities*   50
- *Spot Built Homes*   52
- *Golf and Resort Homes*   54
- *Senior and All Age Apartments*   57
- *Manufactured Homes*   58
- *Time Sharing Opportunities*   59
- *Assisted Care Living*   60

Chapter Six	Where Do We Start?	69
Chapter Seven	Can We Believe the New Home Sales Pitch?	79
Chapter Eight	Review of The Eighteen Decision Factors	85

1. *Can We Stay Where We Are?*   86
2. *Which Type of Residence?*   88
3. *The Children and Grandkids*   90
4. *Doctors, Butchers, Bakers*   91
5. *Community Location*   93
6. *The Size of the Community*   95

7. *Clubhouses, Recreation and Amenities*   98
8. *Homeowners Associations/Fees*   102
9. *Security Considerations*   106
10. *Home Quality, Design, Price, and*   108
       — All Those Options
11. *Job Market. Will I work?*   128
12. *Resale Market Forecast*   130
13. *Health Considerations*   132
14. *Should I Buy a Resale Home?*   133
15. *Estate Planning*   134
16. *Mortgages*   136
17. *Real Estate Taxes*   139
18. *Am I Too Old To Do This?*   141

Chapter Nine   **Prioritizing Factors**   143
Chapter Ten   **Micro Analysis of Your Choice(s)**   155
Chapter Eleven   **Making the Decision to Buy**   163

Part II — After the Purchase

Chapter Twelve   **Purchase Agreements and Contingencies**   171
Chapter Thirteen   **Selling the Old House-- the Choices**   189
   • *The Market Has Changed*   190
   • *Resale Market Realities*   194
   • *Agency Relationships*   200
   • *FSBO--Is It Worth the Risks?*   203
   • *Broker Referrals*   206
   • *Getting The House Ready and Repairs*   209
Chapter Fourteen   **Proper Real Estate Brokerage**   213
Chapter Fifteen   **Home Selling Assistance**   217
Chapter Sixteen   **It's Sold— Now What?**   223
Chapter Seventeen   **There's Lawyers and There's Lawyers**   227
Chapter Eighteen   **The Transition Period**   233
Chapter Nineteen   **Moving Considerations**   239
Chapter Twenty   **Socializing in Your New Home**   251
Chapter Twenty-One   **What Would I Have Done Differently?**   259

Book Order Form   269
Community Profiles   271

INTRODUCTION

For the past three years, I have spoken to thousands of senior real estate prospects who have been actively searching for a house and community in which to spend their golden retirement years.

You would think that with so many contacts with people of the same age and demographic profile that we would be able to determine some common factors and concerns that could be of use to others in the same category that are about to embark on this major purchase of a new or resale home. Well, the happy news is that we can.

Senior buyers that are looking for active adult communities and retirement facilities have many common characteristics that are outlined below for your review. They fall into categories that are financial, psychological, or physical and are generally consistent from one couple or individual buyer to the next.

Before we begin our planning process, I want you to read through the following list and see if your feelings, concerns and fears match those of others of the same age that are beginning the same search and investigation into the purchase of a senior residence.

Typical Active Adult Buyer (s) (Is this you?)

Are between the ages of 50 and 80. Average 66.

Have been in home an average of 27 years.

Have grown children with grandchildren.

"Think" they are sure of which state to live in.

Don't want to maintain big home and yard anymore.

Feel that their town has changed around them.

State that friends have already moved or are gone.

Typically have little debt and the house is paid in full.

Does not want to have a mortgage if at all possible.

Is skeptical of real estate brokers and salespeople.

Is thinking about scaling down to one car from two.

Is concerned about health of self and/or spouse.

Wants to get the other spouse settled ASAP.

Is concerned about the children's travel time to them.

Don't know if they will find good doctors nearby.

Are unsure of their recreational needs.

Is afraid of the "retirement city" image.

Has just recently or is about to stop working.

May want to find part-time work after moving in.

Has at least one dependent parent to contend with.

Feels guilty about spending money on themselves.

Is unsure about how much a new house should cost.

Is unsure about listing price for their current house.

Considers property taxes a primary consideration.

Feels that a clubhouse should meet their needs.

Overestimates the importance of a clubhouse.

Is unsure of their spouses "real" social desires.

Has family furniture that they "cannot" part with.

Has closets and basements that are over flowing.

Is dreading the entire moving (and cleaning) process.

Is unsure about the planned community "lifestyle."

Is overly cautious in the presence of salespeople.

Will visit and re-visit many retirement communities.

Will delay decision to purchase as long as possible.

Visits the best communities four times before buying.

Feels guilty about buying too many options.

Will rely on the children's input too much.

Will try and find reasons why they shouldn't buy now.

Have not reached a decision on "snowbird" lifestyle.

Have not travelled widely throughout the USA.

Probably don't know a real estate attorney.

Will overestimate the value of their home.

Will listen to information and education if presented.

Has faced one recent health problem of concern.

Has a house full of memories to deal with.

Wants to make all the furniture fit into the new home.

Hasn't had time for a hobby or non-work interest.

I think you've gotten the picture. Most of the people in the adult marketplace are a lot like you.

In preparing ***Our Old House—Our New Home***, I have kept activity steps in a logical order of occurrance. Chapter One topics happen first, Chapter Two topics happens second and so on. You should first read the entire book in chronological order. But, after that you can return to individual chapters as necessary to study a topic that is of most current interest or that you want to understand more fully while you are experiencing it in the real field condition.

My intent is to make you the smartest customer possible. This will make your research time more efficient and will also alert the professionals that you come into contact with that you are a saavy buyer who knows the important questions. And, by the way, don't settle for salespeople or realtors that you don't like or that don't treat you with respect. The good ones will listen to you —if you listen to them. So be optimistic and open but don't let a bad salesperson waste your time. If they resist your thorough approach to the purchase, ask for a new salesperson.

I've included my phone number and E-Mail address at the end of this book for you to contact me if you have any questions. Remember that different states around the country may have different legal or contract requirements, sales tax or value added taxes, or special regulations regarding age-restricted communities. For your safety and financial security, please rely on your attorney for any legal advice and your accountant for any questions relating to finances.

— Best of Luck.

PART I

PREPARING FOR

THE PURCHASE

WE THINK IT'S TIME TO LEAVE

I was talking to John and Grace last week in my realty office at an active adult community and, as I usually do, I asked them why they were leaving their neighborhood where they had spent the past forty-three years.

They looked over at each other for a brief second and told me in unison, " It's time."

With increases in populations to previously "small" towns, the character and atmosphere that once drew married couples to purchase their first homes in these areas has now changed to the point of being uncomfortable. People don't feel as safe and secure as they once did when life was simple and residents weren't required to lock front doors and could leave garage doors wide open without fear of unwanted visitors.

Progress and people do change towns and cities. And sometimes it is best just to move on rather than to become recluses in your own home — content to ignore what is going on around you. Add to that the changes in family, health, and financial conditions, and the ending of work careers, and you begin to see a myriad of reasons why seniors sometimes reluctantly start the retirement home search.

Below, I have recounted some actual buyer reasons that have been cited to me over the last several years. I think you'll see that many match your own.

• Most of our friends have moved, retired, or passed away. We are alone and our social life has stopped.

• The children have grown and moved to other parts of the state or country. We have to fly to see them.

• The house is just too big for the two of us. We're lost in it. And it takes me forever to clean it.

• I don't want (my husband) to mow the lawn anymore. We can't pay attention to the yard like we did when we were younger.

• The people moving into town are not our typical style. We don't like the types of people moving here.

• The house will need extensive (and expensive) repairs if we stay. We'll never recover it if we sell later.

• We can't go up and down the stairs anymore.

• My husband (wife) has a heart condition. There is just too much work to do around here.

• We want a simple house we can " lock and leave" easily. We want to travel and have some fun.

• The crime rate in our area has risen sharply this past year. Our neighbor was robbed one month ago.

• The traffic in our town has become unbearable.

• We want to be near people our own ages and make new friends. We aren't working anymore.

• I want to get into a community where my spouse will be safe if something happens to me.

• The real estate market is as good as it has been in ten years. If we sell now we will get the best price for our home.

• My spouse passed away a few years ago and the house I'm in has too many memories. I want to move on.

• We're both retired and no longer commute to work ten minutes away. We are now free to go anywhere we want.

• The weather has been awful up here. We want to get out of the bad winters.

• We need a structure for our retirement social life. We want to be near people with whom we can share common interests and activities.

• We can't afford to live on our fixed income without taking a profit on our large home and buying a smaller retirement home.

• Our friends moved down to a retirement community and they love it. We want to share in the fun too.

• My children (or grandchildren) live where we are looking and they want us to be closer to them.

• We've had a good life but realize that we only have a small window of living left. We want to spend the next twenty years or whatever we are blessed with in a comfortable, social, and safe community. We are searching for a relaxed and carefree retirement.

• My wife thinks it is best to move to a more manageable place. I'm not sure yet, but I'll look.

• My husband always wanted to learn to play golf. Now he will be able to give it a try.

Whatever your reasons for deciding to make investigation into the retirement housing market, you will need to make a plan for your research if you are to make the right choice.

We will now provide you with a recommended way to proceed successfully. If you and your spouse take your time and plan your effort wisely, you will be months ahead of your friends and will probably decide to counsel them on their home purchase after you are well settled in your new home.

A PLAN FOR RESEARCHING THE MOVE

Now that you have decided that you want to explore all of the possibilities of moving to a retirement community or facility, you are faced with a lot of confusion as to the best way to proceed.

Friends will tell you one thing, the radio and television another, and the newspapers and magazines are filled with plenty of "glamourous" ads stating that one place is better than another. Some ads will even offer thousands of dollars of savings if you will favor one community over another.

You need a plan of action if you are to make a sensible decision based upon facts and not marketing entrapment. You'll also need a quarterback to get you to the goal line in the most efficient manner. In this and subsequent chapters, we will endeavor to provide you with a twelve step plan that will be logical and easy to follow and reward you with saved time, less aggravation, and perhaps the best final decision you can make.

The following chart will summarize our 12 Step planning and purchasing procedure. In Part I of **Our Old House** your activities within the individual boxes will be fully defined. Go at your own pace.

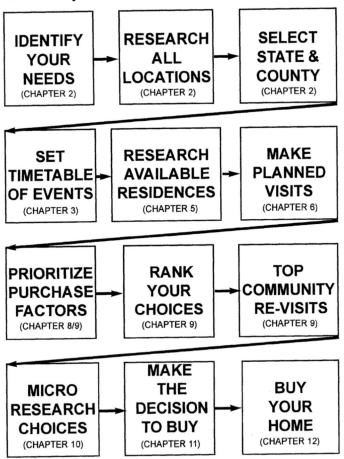

IDENTIFY YOUR NEEDS (CHAPTER 2) → RESEARCH ALL LOCATIONS (CHAPTER 2) → SELECT STATE & COUNTY (CHAPTER 2)

SET TIMETABLE OF EVENTS (CHAPTER 3) → RESEARCH AVAILABLE RESIDENCES (CHAPTER 5) → MAKE PLANNED VISITS (CHAPTER 6)

PRIORITIZE PURCHASE FACTORS (CHAPTER 8/9) → RANK YOUR CHOICES (CHAPTER 9) → TOP COMMUNITY RE-VISITS (CHAPTER 9)

MICRO RESEARCH CHOICES (CHAPTER 10) → MAKE THE DECISION TO BUY (CHAPTER 11) → BUY YOUR HOME (CHAPTER 12)

"Researching The Move"

<u>**12 Step Purchasing Activity Chart**</u>

(time to complete all steps — 6 to 18 months)

If you are married, it will be imperative that you communicate fully with your spouse throughout your decision process. Honesty and open dialogue will focus your interests, save you time and prevent aggravation. Without cooperation, you will flounder.

I am consistently amazed to see the interaction between senior couples that have thrived over the course of their marriages. Those that have maintained their own individual personalities and identities without sacrificing the integrity of the "couple" are indeed rare entities today. And they are to be congratulated.

I dwell on this phenomenon because I want the reader to understand that if you DO NOT have a highly honest and communicative relationship with your spouse, you will probably not survive the search for a retirement community or residence. The likelihood is that you will not move at all.

That sounds harsh, I know. But it is true.

In the course of a typical Saturday at an adult community sales office, I may speak to eight or ten couples who are deeply into "the Search" for a retirement dwelling. They will of course vary in personality, financial ability, health, and personal traits. But they are alike in so many other ways that I can almost predict which ones will be able to make a decision to buy and who will just go on to the next community and then the next and never make the purchase decision.(I call them hand "wringers.")

So, before we begin **Step One** of the process of searching for the ideal community or residence for you and your loved one, I want to encourage you to have a very serious but relaxed meeting of the minds with your wife, husband or significant other.

If you are to proceed intelligently, you and your spouse have to talk about some painful issues that may impact where you buy. Retirement lifestyle, hobbies, money, health, fears of loss of the other, family ties and relationships to spouses and grandchildren all have to be discussed so that you can begin the process of identifying your needs.

Many husbands have never discussed their finances with their wives. This must now change.

Many partners have never described their real health condition to their spouses. This must now change. It's time to get it all out on the table.

You must honestly review these issues and prepare an assessment of your mental, financial and physical condition BEFORE you begin your intensive home search.

Let's now begin reviewing the activity steps in our chart on page 18. We will start with the all-important —**IDENTIFICATION OF YOUR NEEDS.**

Step 1— IDENTIFY YOUR NEEDS

If I am in need of constant care and cannot feed myself, I will most certainly have my decision as to where I live made by others. I will undoubtedly be in a nursing home.

If my wife and I have never played golf in our lives and have no interest in taking up the sport, we most certainly will not buy in an adult community which has a golf course that must be paid for by home-owners association dues.

If we are lucky enough to be independently wealthy and have no obligations to provide support to anyone else and have no children or grandchildren, then we most certainly will consider purchasing an all -year suite aboard a new Swedish Sailing vessel for about $1,400,000 plus gratuities.

Our first step in determining where we will look for our retirement home requires an honest assessment of our physical, financial, mental, marital, familial, and recreational needs. When these requirements are identified, we may begin the research process.

The following questions are the critical issues that you will have to address before you go visiting adult communities or assisted care facilities. These are sensitive issues and will take a few nights for you both to be on the "same page" when it comes time to make decisions about your future home. I suggest you go out for a quiet dinner, return home and get each other familiar with your TRUE facts and feelings. Use the following topics as "thought triggers."

You and your spouse **must** discuss:

• What is our exact financial condition?
>   Cash, stocks, annuities, CD's, 401K
>   Debt, loans, mortgages, credit cards
>   Assets, home, cars, property, etc.
>   Loans receivable from others
>   Insurance policies (amt./beneficiaries)
>   Personal credit histories
>   Businesses owned financial status
>   Tax status and payments due
>   Ability to qualify for a mortgage

• How is our current and projected health?
>   Past illnesses that could reoccur
>   Recent physical exam results
>   Susceptibility to flus and viruses
>   Sensitivity to the sun
>   Medications taken and reasons
>   Weight and muscle tone condition

• What things do we like to do together?
>   Dance
>   Sports, beach, fishing
>   Theatre, cultural activities
>   Go to dinner
>   Meet with friends socially
>   Visit national parks, volunteer, etc.

- What do I think my SPOUSE likes to do?
  (This will get interesting.)

- What do I like to do alone?
  (Also will be interesting.)

- What family will we miss if we move?
  Will they survive if we relocate?
  How often do we see them now?

- Am I a social person?

- Is my spouse a social person?

- Will we work part-time after we move?

- What are our biggest fears about moving to a
  new place at our age?
  Not making friends?
  Getting sick with only new doctors?
  Missing my grandchildren?
  Moving then losing my spouse?
  Missing my old house?
  Not liking my new home?
  Missing my friends?
  Hating the "adult community lifestyle?"
  Feeling "Old " among older people?
  Getting lost in a big adult "city?"
  Not finding stores that I like?
  The whole moving experience?
  Temporary housing and storage?

- What part of the Country will be best?
    Access to the children?
    Feeling of remoteness?
    Disassociation from friends and family?

- Can we still handle a big home?
    The yard duties?
    The snow plowing?
    The stairs and clutter of basements?
    Lack of security or planned activities?

- How much travelling will we be doing?
    Where do we each want to go?

- What do we think about renting?
    One place or several places?
    Could we tolerate apartment living?

- Do we want to be snowbirds?

- Will this purchase affect our estate planning?
    Are we spending the kid's inheritance?

- Will our house be easy to sell?
    Does it needs a lot of repairs?
    Are there a lot of homes for sale nearby?
    Is it neat, clean, and orderly?

- Can we survive the whole moving process?
    Cleaning and repairing the house?
    Yard sales to get rid of stuff?
    Packing and moving men?
    Temporary storage, and housing?

• Where are we sure we **DON'T** want to go?

• What have we specifically heard from friends about actual adult communities or residences?
    (Discuss the features and each spouses reaction to that feature.)

• What family or friends have actually moved?
    Into adult communities?
    Into assisted care living?
    Into other categories being considered?

• What "horror stories" has each spouse heard about active adult living or other facilities being considered?

• What cultural and religious facilities MUST we be nearby at our new place of residence?

With the above and your own questions and concerns addressed and discussed by each spouse in turn (with the other listening) you will develop a good sense of the type of senior facility that should be researched and visited. Honesty now will work best.

For purpose of example, I will review the decision process of Barbara and Sydney, both 61 years old who are just starting to look for their retirement residence. The profile that follows is typical of many of you and you may indeed come to the same conclusions that they did. What I would like to do is review their thinking process in Step One of our chart to show you how they have identified their primary needs at this beginning point of their search.

But first, a little about Barbara and Sydney:

Ages: Both 61 years young.
Previous Occupations:
        Sydney: Phone Company Middle Mgr.
        Barbara: School Administrator
Children: three; with four grandchildren (4-9)
Large home on one acre. Two stories high.
Have limited travel experience. Mostly south.
Want to stay near their kids.
Still have one parent living nearby.
Sydney had a heart scare last year.
Think they want to scale down to one car.
Barbara thought she might work a bit longer.

Barbara and Sydney, in reviewing the factors in the previous pages of this chapter have decided the following regarding their particular needs for a retirement home choice. Some of their concerns are not addressed yet and will only be known after they begin searching out the available facilities. But they will start with the following key decisions understood.

1. They want to be in a NEW active adult community where their neighbors will be their own age.

2. They want a new house and not a resale.

3. They want to be within a one and a half hour drive from their children.

4. They prefer a community that has a club-house with plenty of activities and social events.

5. They must have a one story ranch home design with enough storage and plenty of room for their furniture. It must be quality built.

6. They are not sure if the community must have a security gate with a guard.

7. The town's property taxes must be in a stable condition so they can predict the yearly increases.

8. They are concerned about the traffic in the immediate area of their new home.

9. Barbara wants to know that shopping and work opportunities will be adequate.

10. They can't spend over $ 140,000 on this home, including the options.

11. They aren't sure if they will take a small mortgage or not. They need some advice.

12. They don't want to pay a lot in monthly maintenance fees because they are going to travel extensively.

13. They don't want to have to rent temporary housing or store furniture while their house is being built. They want to move right into the new home from the old one.

14. They want to move in by the Spring of next year.

15. There must be a good cardiologist nearby for Sydney. And a good hospital too.

16. The rules and regulations of the community must be sensible or they will not buy there.

17. They don't want to be faced with pushy salespeople and will not tolerate anything but the truth from the builder's employees.

18. The monthly carrying charges must be fully covered by their pension and social security incomes.

So then, armed with at least a rough idea of what is important to them, Barbara and Sydney will begin to RESEARCH ALL LOCATIONS that will offer them what they are in search of for their final home purchase. They may change their minds over the course of the search due to new information or deeper insight into their "real" needs. But, that is acceptable. The more they learn and the more they know about each other's ideas for retirement living, the happier they will be after the move.

Step 2— RESEARCH ALL LOCATIONS

An integral part of identifying the needs of the buyer is to establish a national location for the new home. As was the case with Barbara and Sydney, the proximity to the children has overridden the decision to go more than 90 minutes away from their existing home. But this decision must not be made lightly.

Some months back, I was speaking to a couple who shared a story with me that is worth repeating here to prove my point.

Fred and Lois had double purchased expensive retirement homes in an active adult community with their old neighbors who had lived next to them for thirty years. The two couples went to the new community together, loved it and bought within days of each other. Fred and Lois sold their old house quickly and started construction on the new home before their neighbors did. As it turned out, the neighbors couldn't sell their old home before the end of the buying contingency date and could not begin new home construction at all. Their purchase agreement expired and they took the house off of the market and felt that they probably would never move at all.

On a subsequent visit to Fred and Lois' a few months after they had moved in, their friends mentioned that they had travelled to Phoenix Arizona and put a deposit on a home there in a great community where the weather, amenities, taxes, home designs, and clubhouses were beyond belief. They bragged so much that Fred and Lois began to wonder why they hadn't done a little more traveling before making such a permanent retirement decision. They wondered if they shouldn't now put their NEW home on the market and make the move to Arizona with their friends.

After speaking to a few realtors within their new adult community, they soon realized that they would not recover their purchase price because the community was still selling new houses out of the sales office and they had put too many options into the home which most buyers would not want to pay for. They were stuck there at least until the community was sold out. That would be about two more years— a lot when you are 65.

TAKE YOUR TIME.

Travel a bit before you commit to a particular state or region. You may find that you like it better in South Carolina, San Diego, or Atlantic City, New Jersey. You may find that your middle-management children GET TRANSFERRED by their companies and will not be a mere 90 minutes away AFTER you move to your new home.

Think of yourselves FIRST. You are worth the trip if your kids have to get on a plane to see you.

You are worth the trip if they have to drive for half a day to get to you in North Carolina, on the golf course. Try to be a little bit selfish and just consider all the possibilities before you spend $ 150,000 on this next residential purchase.

If you consider all areas, take some trips, and have some fun in the process, you won't have lost anything but time and money. And it may make all the difference in your decision and your ultimate happiness wherever you decide to buy.

Step 3— SELECT STATE AND COUNTY

Since our couple has set the the parameter of not being more than one and one-half hours away from their children and grandchildren, they have marked out a driveable radius of 90 miles from their existing home. That will encompass 18 counties in their home state and three counties in a bordering state where they have visited from time to time.

When visiting adjoining states, make sure to call all communities you will be visiting ahead of time to find out the exact age requirements of residents and children. Some may vary slightly.

The following resources should be relied upon to identify the communities that you will want to visit and accumulate data on utilizing the *Community Checklist / Profiles* in the Appendix of this guide:

Research Resources to Locate Communities

1. Major newspapers in each county and state.
   Friday and Sunday real estate sections
   Sunday supplements
   Community brochures requested by mail
2. Each county's Chamber of Commerce
   Call and ask for names of communities.
3. Each county's Office on Aging or Senior
   Services. Social Services also.
4. National Association of Homebuilders and
   the State Association of Homebuilders.
   Ask for directory of builders who are
   developing senior complexes in the area
   of your interest.
5. Yellow Page directories under Active Adult
   Communities, Residential Developers,
   Assisted Care Living.
6. State Board of Realtors — for list of realtors
7. Major real estate brokers in each county.
8. Town Halls — Town Clerks
9. Local storeowners and shopkeepers.
   As you travel through towns you like.
10. Local township libraries — resource
    books and employees who live in towns.
11. Local and county maps showing communi-
    ties and developments.
12. Friends and family that have moved to
    adult communities. Find out where they
    have looked and what they liked. Did they
    keep their brochures? Don't be shy — Ask.

SET TIMETABLE OF EVENTS

Before proceeding with the actual research of each of your chosen communities, I want to present the following summary which shows the chronological order of key steps in your decision making process. This is **Step Four** on your chart.

By knowing when each step in the process occurs, you will be better prepared to speak with salespeople at the various communities you will visit.

Key to this timetable is your preferred "move-in" date. This is where you (and your spouse) really have to be honest and admit your true timing desire.

The Purchasing Decision Process
— Discussion of retirement and moving to new home
— Sample visits to several retirement communities
— Light discussions with friends and family
— Decision to buy this book and start getting serious
— Decision to leave old house for new home
— **Set date of occupancy. Your move-in date.**
(This date sets up the entire purchase process)

Looking ahead to try and fix a date to move into your new home will be difficult. Procrastination will be easier to accomplish than positive action toward your goal. You may find yourselves thinking about reasons NOT to set a date at all. Here are some typical "stalls" and reasons to delay we frequently hear:

1. "Moving is a pain in the neck ! We'll have to clean up the house and get it ready for sale. It may require too many expenditures on repairs to bring it up to marketable condition. It will be impossible to clean out the closets, basement and the attic. There are just too many memories in the house and there is just too much stuff that we'll have to give away or throw out."

2. "We really love our old house. It's not our fault that we've gotten older and can't do the yard work anymore. It's not our fault that we're not working now and have to start to restrict our expenditures due to our fixed income level. It's not our fault that all of our friends have moved away and the town has changed and the traffic is unbearable. "Why can't it be like it used to be? We loved it just the way it was?"

3. "My wife really wants to move, I don't. If she wasn't pushing for this, we would stay right where we are with our friends, and doctors, and everything just as it is. But, I guess if she wants it, I'll go along."

4. "We're just really looking now. We have plenty of time to make this decision. Our health is

good right now and we may not have to do this for a couple of years yet. We have time."

5. Children frequently add so much pain to the decision because they don't want their parents to move. There may be a new grandchild or one on the way. It's hard to break that tie of caring for your children, at any age.

6. One or both of you may still be working and you either don't want to retire or don't know when your company is going to give you an early release.

7. So many NEW communities are coming onto the scene that you may be afraid to buy for fear you will miss out on the next better community. (You don't realize that prices will be higher the longer you delay the decision.)

8. You wonder what will happen to you if you move and one of you gets sick or dies. What will the other one do? "Will I want to return to my old neighborhood or will I stay because we made the decision to move together?"

I could go on and on. I think you understand that the over fifty-five buyer will have a tendency to delay this purchase for a lot of reasons. But this is good. It can make you a more careful buyer and one that is very certain of their decision when it is finally made. Since it has been my personal sales experience in this market that the typical buyer will visit a community four or five times before placing a deposit, I have learned to make each of these visits count. I begin to talk about the preferred move-in date as early as possible. When buyers learn that builders need four to five months to build their home they start to realize that the process will take longer than they had figured. Once they see this timeline and understand it, it will become apparent that a date MUST be targeted for the approximate desired occupancy. But, please do not feel uncomfortable if you are uncertain about when you REALLY want to move. A good salesperson will guide you through the planning process easily. And a good salesperson will also understand if you decide to stay put and not move at all.

As I indicated, the date of occupancy sets up the entire purchase process that precedes it. Below is the **ORDER** of occurances in your decision to buy a typical retirement home. In a moment you will discover that you must step through the process backwards to determine the date you should PURCHASE your new home.

The Purchase Process *(in order of occurance)*
— Decide to investigate retirement living
— Buy this book
— Identify needs
— Research locations
— Select state
— Set timetable of events
— Research available properties

— Community visits (Your field research)
— Prioritizing personal preference factors
— Qualitative ranking of all communities
— Targeted re-visits to the best communities
— Micro research of the community of choice
— Close estimate on price of home with options
— Reservation deposit on new home
— Agreement of Sale on new home
— Getting the old house repaired / ready for listing
— Selection of real estate broker
— Real estate listing period on old house
— Sale of old house to others
— Legalities leading to closing on old house
— Closing of title on old house
— Release of sale of home contingency with builder
— Release of any mortgage contingency
— The selection process for colors and options
— The construction process (Approx. 5 months)

    The construction process starts at the time of selection of colors and options when you have decided to get the construction of your home underway. The information and option orders are "released" to the construction department and they order a building permit from the township where the home is to be built. The process of getting the building permit can take from one to several weeks depending on the town and the amount of new homes being built at that time. Once the permit is received, the actual construction phases of the home begin. These include pouring of footings, foundations, slabs, crawl spaces or basements, framing, sheathing, plumbing, electrical, roofing, siding, flooring, appliances, insulation, interior finishes, painting, installation of fireplaces, and all other construction activities that you are more than likely familiar with. During the building process, all of the needed township inspections occur to make sure that your home is being built in accordance with the various codes that exist. Some builders have planned inspections for the buyer too so that he or she can see the home being built and be assured of the quality level on a more intimate basis.

— The Certificate of Occupancy
— Final inspection of your home before closing
— Closing of title (day before or day of moving in)
— Moving Day— You move into your NEW home

As you plan your purchase, you will find it useful to reverse the above process to arrive at the optimum time to place your reservation deposit and actually BUY your home. The process of working backward from the occupancy date is critical for you in picturing WHEN you have to move to action. For example, lets say that Barbara and Sydney from the last chapter want to move in on September 1, of the year 2000. If they have a house to sell, their reverse timeline would look something like the following:

— September 1, 2000 — Move into NEW home
— April 1, 2000 — Selections /construction release
— March 20, 2000 -Release sale of home contingency

— March 15, 2000 — Closing on old house
— Complete legalities of selling old house (60 days)
— House is sold January 15th, 2000 (75 days)
— November 1, 1999 — List house with broker
— October 1, 1999 — Broker search / home repair
— September 29, 1999 — Agreement of Sale
— September 22, 1999 — Reservation Deposit
— 3 to 18 months prior— Researching the move

As you can see, not counting all of your research and community visiting time, you are looking at about a year-long process from beginning to end if you have a home to sell before starting your new residence. If you don't have a home to sell or are purchasing with just a mortgage contingency, the timetable will be reduced by about three to five months. In any event, you can see the reason to plan ahead. There will be a lot of things to do and each step will require different input from a variety of people.

Very often I will be speaking to a new customer for the first time and I will ask them when they picture themselves moving. I am always amazed when they say in October that they would like to move in the spring. With a house to sell, it's NOT going to happen, folks. It's physically impossible.

I would like to interject a personal thought here. I believe that the person you are buying the home from should be able to help you through the timing process and answer a lot of your questions about how and

when to do certain things. Very often, we are intimi-
dated in the presence of fast talking salespeople and
don't get what we deserve in the way of information.
I urge you to demand it. You deserve to understand
every detail you feel is important before you buy.
Trust your instincts and ask. If you can't get satisfaction from one salesperson, then ask the manager for
another.

ASKING (TELLING) THE KIDS

I wasn't sure whether or not I should devote a whole chapter of this book to the topic of children. After all, this is about you, right— not your kids.

As a sales counselor in an active adult community in the Northeast, you can imagine that one of my first questions to prospective buyers is " Why have you decided to stay up here in this weather when you could just as easily relocate to Arizona, Florida, Texas or any one of ten other great and warm locations?"

Answers will undoubtedly include references to children and grandchildren who are high on the priority list when it comes to the decision to purchase a retirement home. As Americans, we have a strong sense of family and never seem to stop caring for our own. Even if it means neglecting our own needs and desires in the process. And, this too extends to our aging parents as well. Many times a purchase has been delayed or passed on because of a mother or father who is still living with the couple or who is in a nursing home and needs constant attention. That

kind of situation seems to be tougher than leaving
children behind because we are not yet used to living
longer than our parent's generation. Moms and Dads
in their late nineties are no longer a rarity. We must
adjust.

Last month, a couple came into my office for
the sixth or seventh time and told me that they finally
had convinced their 88 year old mother to agree to a
double home purchase; one for Mom and one for the
two 58 year-old "kids". It seemed unusual and expensive, but the buyers really wanted to get on with their
early retirement and wanted to buy before prices
began to skyrocket.

Well, things seemed to be progressing. Mom
came down and went through the houses and the clubhouse and agreed to the venture. She picked a lot right
next to her children where they could be in easy
earshot if needed. Everyone seemed happy.

Just before the contract was signed, the son
called me up and said that his mother had changed her
mind and that the deal would have to be postponed
indefinitely. What a shame.

In another case, a recently widowed mother of
two came to our community and fell in love with the
homes and the lifestyle and decided to buy. She had
her daughter come down the following week to see the
houses and give her approval. As you can imagine,

some children have agendas of their own and this one was no exception. She stated to me in my office in her mother's presence that " I know my mother and she only sees the options and the new homes and really doesn't want to be here so far away from the rest of her family."

After I spent a futile moment trying to make her understand that her mother had a say in this decision, they both left. Her mother was very obviously upset by the outburst. We both were aware that this was "babysitter loss" syndrome and nothing more. The mother called me a few days later and said that she would be down soon to give her reservation deposit.

In my work at adult communities, I have developed a thick skin while listening to some children of seniors. I am compassionate with the situation but normally tell this to the parents when we are alone:

" It's obvious that you and your children have a close relationship and that they rely on you for counsel, assistance, and help when they need it. This is as it should be in any family. But, you are at the stage of your lives when it is YOUR TIME to do with as you please. For the last forty years you have tended to the financial, physical, and mental needs of your kids. Well, guess what, they're grown up now and you aren't always going to be here to help them. So maybe it's time to lengthen the embilical chord a bit and do it your way for a change. We're only here for a visit.

It's time they gave you a break and let you have some relaxation and fun on your own terms."

Other times, we hear about thirty year-olds still living at home, unmarried and living off of their parents. I know they are loved and Mom wants to stand by them. But, I say kick them out (nicely). It will be best for them and it will let you get on with your lives. Of course, from time to time a divorce or injury may require you to help out. But, that has to be temporary, for your well being. This is your time now. Be firm.

The following brief chart will be enough for you to understand the need for some real decisions regarding the kids. **MOST KIDS ARE GREAT**, but a few are really only thinking about their own convenience.

If <u>they</u> <u>say</u>:	They mean:
You'll be too far away, the granchildren will miss you.	Who will we have to babysit ?
It's not prudent financially. You love your old house. There's all those memories of us growing up.	Keep your money invested in tax free municipals. It's our inheritance. We have some rights too.
It will be too exhausting to make a move at your age.	We're too busy to help and we have vacation plans.
Why don't you fix up the old house. It'll be great.	Babysitter and Inheritance concerns. Same old song.
The move will be too hard on Dad. Think of him.	Why don't you think about us anymore, Mom?

Chapter Five

REAL ESTATE COMMUNITY CHOICES

This chapter relates to **Step Five— Researching Available Facilities** on your Purchasing Activity Chart on Page 18. Here, we will outline the types of residential opportunities that are available to the entire market so you will not be surprised later on in your search. While you have already selected a type of facility when you identified your needs, this section will be your reference for the choices to select from. Chapter Six will review starting your actual site visits.

As it stands in today's realty and health-care world, the following is a suggested list of retirement housing choices. We will review the major ones that you are most likely to be considering and discuss some important features of each type:

— Existing Retirement Communities
— Active Adult Communities
— All-Age Communities
— Spot Built Homes
— Golf and Resort Developments

— Senior Apartments
— All-Age Apartments
— Manufactured Home Parks
— Time-Share Opportunities
— Assisted Care Living
— Mixed Use Assisted Living

In Chapter Two we outlined the many factors you will be considering in identifying your needs for your retirement home. That will be a continuing process as you begin to make visits and learn more about each type of location and style of living.

Important factors that will come up again and again as you determine these needs will be the following which will focus your decision to one category or another after you prioritize your needs later on.

In reviewing all of these following types of lifestyles, keep in mind:

— Your physical condition and health
— Your need for special services
— Your need for privacy
— Your need for healthcare services
— Your need for security
— Your need for transportation services
— Your need for social interaction
— Your need for individuality
— Your financial flexibility
— Your degree of pride in ownership
— Your insurance and estate planning needs

Existing Retirement Communities

Some thirty years ago, large developers in an effort to house the ever growing population of "senior citizens", as they were called, began to build large-scale retirement villages for the 65 year-old and over retirement buyer. At that time, needs were simple and home designs were primarily suited to fixed income and low activity buyers. People were not as healthy as they are today. They were not living as long either. And, consequently, their demands allowed for smaller floorplans, less closet space, and very modest amenities.

Since the bulk of today's senior aged buyer is more affluent than their predecessors and since they are in better physical health due to improvements in medicine, physician care, and general attitude toward diet and fitness, the "older" senior communities have not been an attractive purchasing alternative for them.

Typical 1960 home designs were in the 1100 to 1300 square foot ranch style and today are reselling in the $ 60,000 to $ 95,000 range. While there are plenty of them for sale, the current market is only attracting buyers with limited financial capability or six month "snowbirds" who just need a base of operations with little concern for luxury. Even updated units with expanded kitchens and addition of sunrooms are only selling in the $ 100,000 to $ 120,000 range.

During the 1980's, senior communities began adding expanded designs, more model choices, larger lots, more purchase options and modest clubhouses for community use. But, in comparison to the active adult communities of the 1990's, they are dwarfed in both appeal and prospective buyer demand. They too, like the earlier versions, are only appealing to the buyers with tighter financial constraints and the "north-south" two home retiree.

Active Adult Communities

The senior community of the 1990's mirrors the best of resort living and the most modern and maintenance-free home designs ever imagined. Coined "ACTIVE ADULT LIFESTYLE COMMUNITIES," each one seems to be trying to out do the other in sizes of clubhouses, types of amenities, number of home-sites, and quality of living.

While sizes of these exciting new venues can range from a few hundred to a few thousand, they all have certain features in common:

- Maintenance free, one level home designs
- One or two car garages
- Grass cutting and snow removal services
- Well appointed clubhouses and amenities
- Modest building lot sizes. (50 x 100)
- Premium lot availability
- Wide range of structural home options

- Wide range of interior design options
- Wide range of convenience options
- Energy saving options
- Organized Homeowners Association
- Planned association social calendar
- Manned or mock guard houses
- Attractive sales and design center on site
- Lakes, fountains, attractive retention ponds
- 10 to 15 year homeowner's warranties
- Well equipped standard features
- Monthly maintenance fee for services
- Few allowed structural changes to plans
- Quality but medium grade building materials
- Plethora of association activity committees
- Recreation director may or not be employed
- Age restricted to 55 and over
- No children allowed under 19
- Nearby attractions and recreation activities
- Community bus service
- Many county senior services provided
- Outside training in hobbies and crafts
- Some have visiting medical services
- Strict rules and regulations to be followed

Many new active adult communities are allowing a percentage of under 55 buyers who may be retiring early or that may have several homes around the country. Each community will have its own legal position on this allowance and may or may not have it reported in its literature. You will have to ask.

With the heavy emphasis on recreational amenities, many new communities are adding golf courses
to their site to attract the recreational and country club
golfer to their community. Both executive (under
6000 yards in length) and regulation Par 72 courses
are being built and may or may not be open to the public. Usually, if they are public, the residents will have
a preferred tee time schedule or will be given a price
discount or advanced reservation advantage.

As we come to the turn of the century, we must
ask ourselves if the trend toward the larger communities will continue or if the recent movement to smaller
more elegant developments will prevail. With so
many of us reaching age 50, it is likely that there will
be demand enough for all types and sizes for facilities.
And, as always, the style, price, and amenities offered
will significantly depend on the availability of suitable
and affordable land parcels that can be efficiently
developed in light of today's stringent political and
environmental conditions.

All-Age Communities

Real estate is booming all over the country and
Americans are in a very prosperous time. Mortgage
rates are low and most 55 year old retirees can live
ANYWHERE they want.

Distinctions in the marketplace between the 55
to 60 year-old buyer and the 60 and over buyer must

be made. But, the motivation of a young retiree couple to choose the " protective" and easy lifestyle of an active adult community over a beautiful new all-age community will probably come down to the following factors:

1. Are they unrestricted in their financial capability? Will they hire services?
2. Do they prefer a "custom built" home?
3. Do they want top grade construction materials?
4. Do they have security concerns?
5. How many cars will they have to garage?
6. Do they require "structured" social activity?
7. Are they very "individualistic?"
8. Will they be working out of their home?
9. Can they live with the loss of privacy?
10. Do they have a concern for "status?"
11. Do they have physical liabilities?
12. Will they have more than one home?
13. Do they want to risk "noisy neighbors?
14. Are their children's wishes a concern?
15. Might their parents eventually live with them if they became unable to care for them selves?
16. Do they want to care for a large home?

While all-age communities are plentiful, popular and beautiful, most will agree it appears that the appeal wanes as the affluent 55 year-old becomes 60. It is only an option for the lucky few seniors who want to hang on to their independence for a while longer.

Spot Built Homes

There is a faction of senior buyers that want a new home in a popular new area of the state or country but who don't want to pay more than they "think" the new community home is worth. This buyer is typically on a restricted budget where they will have little money left over after the sale of their existing home and must conserve as much as possible on the new home purchase. Often, they feel that the cost of amenities and attractive entryways of today's new communities are being added to the price of the home and they resist this concept.

The "spot-built" home is sometimes the chosen alternative of this buyer. It is the same for a senior buyer as it is for a first-time buyer. The home is built by a small local builder who has several speculation building lots in the area that he has been holding for just such a purpose. There are no amenities, no social lifestyle, no apparent advantages except that the same square footage home that was available in the adult community may cost a few thousand dollars less if built in this manner. There may also be more flexibility to add closets, rooms, special material or product selections, and rear yard options.

For most of these renegade senior buyers, the customer profile looks something like the following:

— Buyer thinks community home prices are
  too high
— Has resistance to rules and regulations
— Wants to make structural changes to the
  house that the builder won't approve
— Thinks options are priced too high
— Are not interested in the social life
— Wants privacy and independence
— Wants fences, sheds, and vegetable gardens

These buyers will often come into the adult community time and time again and take measurements of the model they like and continue to press the salesperson for changes and accommodations and price reductions only to eventually give up and go their separate ways. It is probable that they try and get the spot builder to replicate the active adult home but likely back away from that because architect's plans will have to be produced and could lead to infringement ramifications for the architect.

This buyer, while over 55, is really not a part of the marketplace for active adult homes. Rather, he is just an older buyer who still wants his own private space.

They choose to cut their own grass, shovel their own snow, and tell their neighbors how much money they saved by NOT moving to the new adult community down the street. For some, the right solution. For others, senior isolationism — and a shame.

Golf and Resort Developments

In the warmer regions of the country there has grown up some very exciting resort oriented communities that boast golf courses, water sports, restaurants, shopping, lifestyles of the rich and famous and amenities that will suit every taste that exists. Such places are found in Arizona, North Carolina, Florida, Georgia, South Carolina and other great states. They are truly destination retirement choices for those that can afford the prices and who have the flexibility to leave their roots and families in the east, mid-west, or other parts of the United States.

Researching these locations will be fun vacations for sure, but buyers must be careful not to be lured into purchasing before they are ready. For sometimes, while on vacation and very relaxed, we can be swayed by effective sales presentations and can find ourselves putting down deposit monies that we will later be trying to recover in court.

I believe that a move to a far away resort styled retirement community is for the carefree that do not have ties to family and grandchildren rather than for the rest of us. But it is an option and you may want to consider it. Why not plan a trip with another couple?

As has been the case in Florida for decades, developers in many states are now trying their hand at golf communities even if not in the hotter climates.

They are counting on the recent increase in popularity of the game of golf and are hoping that some of the retirees that have been relocating to Florida can be convinced to stay in their home state and still get the flavor of the golf community lifestyle.

The success of these communities to date has been mixed. Some have worked and others have not. The ones that have worked best thus far have done one of two things. In the first case they have combined two developers in the project; one for the housing and another for the golf course design, development, and management. It seems that you cannot be all things to all men. Either be a builder of homes or a builder of golf courses. If you try to do it all, it doesn't seem to work. The second case where it has worked especially well for senior communities is to combine an "executive golf course" with the master planned housing community. Here a scaled down course of nine or eighteen holes can be played quickly and is not overly expensive to build because it is devoid of expensive greens and bunker complexes and is more for a friendly game of iron play rather than a regulation Par 72 event.

As a senior home buyer and a senior golfer, you must decide if the convenience of having a course on site is important enough to you and your wife to compensate for the usually higher maintenance fee to maintain its playability. Golf courses can be very expensive and most regulation courses require

$500,000 and more as a yearly maintenance budget. You must also consider the way that seniors like to play golf. Typically, they will play with the same three or seven players each week and it is fun to try different places for a change of scenery. Golfers like the variety of many different types of venues and may be bored playing an executive course over and over.

In summary, it can be assumed that the purchasers of homes in all-age golf communities with regulation courses will be affluent and between 30 and 55 years old. They do not require the social amenities of an adult community because they enjoy that at the country club setting they have bought into.

The active adult communities that have golf courses will only attract buyers if they control the cost of maintenance of the golf course by making it executive style only or a regulation course that is also open to the public to offset its high cost of operation. While seniors are supposed to love golf, they will not pay for it unless it is reasonably priced. Imagine the wife of a golfing husband that is spending $ 140 per month for a golf facility that she doesn't use. And further imagine how they will feel if he is suddenly told by his doctor that he shouldn't play golf anymore because of an eye problem. I think the message is clear. And developers should think this amenity through completely before putting it into their preliminary site plans and presenting it at the public planning board hearings.

Senior and All-Age Apartments

Many of us can remember what it was like when we first got married and moved into that small apartment. We were happy and didn't really mind the poor condition of the building, the leaky window, the inadequate heating system, the hot water that wasn't really hot, the small refrigerator, the creaky stairs, the smell from the downstairs apartment, the noisy neighbor and the closet door that never could be found in the musty basement. Gosh, it was awful.

Apartments haven't come too far for the most part. The first years are always nice. Then the landlord never really seems to care anymore. Things go downhill and we move somewhere else.

I don't ever like to see senior citizens in all-age apartments. I know that there are a lot of you out there but I have heard too many stories about the problems that seniors have with younger tenants, and the noise, and parties. I want you to find a better way if you can.

Senior apartments with special services such as on-site cleaning and shopping and minimal medical nurse services are beginning to spring up as free-standing complexes or in mixed-use communities. As with any purchase decision, you will have to weigh the cost of renting against the cost of buying. First you will have to find these senior apartments. Then you will have to do the math and see if it's right for you.

Manufactured Homes

Factory produced pre-fabricated homes are available today in a wide selection of designs and sizes. Their popularity has increased at a good rate in the senior population because of the purchase price advantage over some of the more expensive active adult communities that are springing up.

Aside from the construction materials and the method of delivery and foundation detail, the actual living space offered is not that different from some of the simpler designs in the "stick built" selection of homes.

Today's manufactured home communities have amenities such as clubhouses, tennis courts, pools and other outdoor facilities and are only dissimilar to their larger cousins in the elaborateness of the site.

A key difference in a manufactured home is that typically you will not own the land under your unit but will rather rent it from the developer of the community. Land rents can cost up to $ 500 per month and will also include your common charges and maintenance.

You may spend ten or fifteen thousand dollars less for a quality pre-fabricated modular, so you should investigate any new community in your chosen area and attend one of the open houses that are frequently held. You may be surprised at what you see.

Time-Share Retirement

Last year, I was on vacation in Mexico and was sitting in a hotel lobby waiting for a time share seminar to start. The couple next to me was in their late sixties and we began to talk about the time share experience. I mentioned that I had a week which I purchased at Hilton Head Island, South Carolina. They said they had one there too. I mentioned that I had booked my current week in Mexico through a time share exchange company. They said that they owned their own week here in Mexico too. This begged for a question. I asked them how many time share weeks they had. They looked at each other and began to recount all of the places where they owned weeks. They told me that they had 26 timeshare weeks that they had purchased around the globe. Twenty-six !

Obviously, they like to travel. And obviously, they have the money to purchase these timeshares. But, it certainly is an interesting way to retire.

They told me that they spent most of the summers with their children and grandchildren in Chicago. But come September they headed out for anywhere they wanted to for as many weeks as they could book. Three weeks in Palm Springs, three weeks in Florida, four weeks in the Carolinas. Back home for holidays, special birthdays and anniversaries. And then back on the road to parts of the world as yet uncharted. Very interesting couple. And, a very interesting retirement.

Assisted Care Living Facilities

Life begins at forty. Or is it really fifty. But now that I'm in good health and nearly sixty — maybe it really begins then. Or what about seventy, the good Lord willing.

We never know how long or how well we will be here on earth. The clock is always ticking. And for some, it strikes midnight much to soon.

We have learned some hard lessons these past several years. We know that we will live longer than our parents. We know that there are some terrible debilitating diseases that rob you of your dignity before your time and over which we have no control. We know that we may outlive our spouse by five, ten, or even fifteen years and we may have to consider the possibility of remarriage, relocation, or re-entry into the part-time work environment. There is a lot of new things to think about. What is the best way for us to plan our "senior future?"

Health should be the number one consideration of us all. For without it no amount of money will be enough to make us happy. We should do everything in our power to keep ourselves and our spouses physically and mentally fit.

Regarding our real estate life planning, we can set ourselves on a couple of different courses of action that may insure that we will be in the right place at the right time and be of as little a burden to our children as possible. But, all of the planning will revolve around two factors — health and money.

The true example that follows may be of interest to you as the type of thinking that a senior may go through as he ages in the 1990's.

Married for 50 years, Joseph and Sarah loved each other dearly. Three children and thirteen grandchildren and a life filled with good luck and prosperity brought them to a point where they were ready to slow down the pace a little and relax. He was 63 and she was 60.

The first year of their decision, Joseph put his son in charge of the family business and he and Sarah went to Florida and rented for three months at a golf course community. They were welcomed immediately, since they both loved golf and soon decided to buy a second home at the same golf course development. They bought a small house with a pool and enjoyed their three month escape yearly for the next two years.

At 66, Joseph developed a medical problem that scared the whole family and he was instructed to retire fully and not even think about shoveling snow again. With regret, he and Sarah decided to buy a bigger place in Florida at the same 3500 home community and move down full time. They built that home and enjoyed it as best they could with Joseph having additional difficulties and a host of doctors appointments throughout the year. They loved the home because Joseph had had a lot of input into the design. (He had designed homes all through their fifty year marriage). But, for Sarah, it was too big and she had a difficult time keeping it the way that SHE wanted to. She decided with Joseph that in light of his health and the size of the house, that they should sell it and get one of the townhouses down the street. They did. And it was quite nice.

A few more years passed. Joseph had some difficulty getting to his upstairs office and was taking a lot of medications for a number of reasons. He didn't even talk about playing golf anymore — a game he loved his whole adult life. His family all knew that his quality of life was slipping and that he was doing his best to keep up but it was only a matter of time.

At the too young age of 74 Joseph died and Sarah was devastated. As were his three children and all of the grandchildren. Sarah was 71 and instructed her children to purchase a townhouse in their home state so she could get out of Florida as soon as possible. She didn't want to even see it. She wanted to get back home where her children were. That was her life now.

Returning home in less than seven weeks, and living in a 2200 square foot two story townhouse, Sarah seemed content enough. But, her children soon learned that she was unhappy and lonely. They had to see her every day so that she would not get depressed. She stayed inside the house most of the day and only ventured out to DRIVE across the street to get groceries. She stayed there for three years and then told her kids that she had had enough. She wanted to go to an assisted care apartment facility on the river four miles away.

Now keep in mind that Sarah had good health, all of her faculties, a loving family that supported her, knew how to drive and had a new car. She was searching for a way to get her identity back before she lost it completely. At that time her children thought that the change itself was the goal rather than a real search for happiness.

Fortunately for Sarah and her three children, the facility she chose to live in was a good one. Of course there were some problems. But, in general, it proved to be the best thing for her at that time.

The key benefits of the facility to Sarah were:
— Safe from crime and personal harm
— Always someone to talk to
— Always someone to give help to
— On-site nurses and doctors if needed
— Full service nursing home when needed
— Hospital services included in fees
— Bus service and social programs
— Sarah knew that her children wouldn't have

to worry about her if she was there at the facility. She wouldn't feel like a burden.

Now two years in the assisted care facility, Sarah has become a bit of a rebel toward the management and food staff. She is the ombudsman on her floor and will complain about things that she feels are wrong for anyone who is too shy to complain themselves. She volunteers on the nursing floor and is always ready to help someone onto or off of the elevator. She is the way she always has been. And, while she entered the facility prematurely some would say, she is living her life the way that she deems best. And therein lies the key to happiness. Know yourself and know what is important to you. Then act guided by your mind and your heart.

Today's choices in assisted care living are just starting to adequately address the needs of the 65 and older buyer who still has a lot of living to do. You must remember that we as a society are just starting to cope with the increased life expectancy of our population. It will take us quite a while to adequately catch up.

Generally the available options include:

— High rise apartments
— Upscale private nursing homes
— Senior campus styled communities
— Mixed use developments

High Rise Assisted Care Apartments

The more apartments that you can get into a building the more profitable it will be for the developer to construct it. Pretty simple concept. Of course, these apartments can be in any configuration. But typically, at least until the last five years, high-rise has seemed to be the preferred style of construction.

Features and Facts:
— Physical exam usually required to get in
— Usually a non-refundable initiation fee
— Relatively high monthly rental
— Full scale nursing floor
— Doctors and nurses on call
— Hospital very near to facility
— Limited common amenities
— Auditorium for lectures
— Cafeteria styled food service
— Slow elevators
— 24 hour security guard
— Inadequate visitor parking
— Low scale unionized work force
— One and two bedroom units typically
— Small square footages
— Kitchenette and one bathroom
— City view out of window
— Outdoor gardens and walking trails
— Shopping within walking distance
— Bus services
— Active yet mild social calendar

Upscale Private Nursing Homes

As the population of America continues to become more affluent, there will continue to be a supplier to fill the demand for any product. Private nursing facilities are no exception. Small, built on wooded parcels with long shaded tree lined drives, these facilities may call themselves resort type names or spas or retreats or rests but they have all of the care and attention that the affluent can afford to grant to themselves or their parents. Prices will begin at the sixty thousand dollar range and move up to $ 100,000 or more annually. They will typically have a group of doctors at the helm and undoubtedly will have a regimined method to good health that includes foods, medicines, vitamins, exercise programs, and regular medical monitoring.

Senior "Campus Styled" Communities

A new type of community has recently been announced and it has some exceptional financial merit that is worth your investigation. It involves the purchase of an apartment for a fixed "price" rather than a non-refundable initiation fee. You still have the substantial monthly maintenance fee (rent) but your full purchase price is refundable to your family or to you on your departure from the facility provided that your unit is resold to a new purchaser.

The amenities offered at the "campus" styled community include lots of senior oriented shopping, full medical facilities and doctors offices, recreational activities found at the best of adult communities, and a host of attractive bike trails and walking trails to help you insure your fitness and peace of mind.

The downside to these communities is that the price of the apartment is about the same as the price of a small home. The square footages may be less that you are accustomed to. And, the number of units is typically in the 2000 to 3000 range, which makes for a lot of neighbors and a lot of political socialization. With the management left to professionals, the owner's group may find itself banding against the establishment if the services don't match up to the promises.

Mixed Use Assisted Care Developments

The most grandeous of senior housing ideas is to construct a complex containing active adult homes, senior apartments, assisted care facilities, medical treatment facilities, and a nursing home.

This sort of one-stop shopping may be the wave of the future, so be on the look out for these. You will have to make your own judgement as to the desirability or need for such a contrived complex. To be successful, one would think it would have to comprise many hundreds of beautiful and well planned acres.

I have spent the time in this chapter to outline the most obvious purchasing choices to you so that you will understand that you indeed DO HAVE CHOICES in your search for a retirement home.

One choice I have not yet mentioned in great detail is the one that you would really prefer to make. That choice is to — STAY WHERE YOU ARE.

Speaking as one who loves the active adult marketplace and the people that make up the buying group (You), I want to just say a few words to you about this choice.

Only you (and your spouse, if you are married) can make the decision to move from your existing house. We have talked about identifying your needs for buying a retirement home. After you finish this book you will almost be an expert on how to go about the thinking process. And that is fine — if you really want to move. But fully review the alternative.

I started the guide by saying that good communication between spouses is critical if you are to get through this process. Use that communication and make up your own minds as to whether you want to renovate your existing house and stay or follow the trends and move to a new place like so many of your friends. Follow your heart and listen to each other. If you decide to make the change, I will help you as much as I can and so will a lot of other people.

WHERE DO WE START ?

In Chapter Three where we discussed setting a Timetable of Events, it was mentioned that the decision to begin to look at the available community options may begin by an innocent visit or two to a newly announced retirement community or active adult community. You and your wife may have been reading the Sunday real estate section and noticed an article about a grand opening of a clubhouse or a NEW section of an existing community. And, like so many other seniors, you may have decided to take a drive.

That was only the beginning. That visit may have peaked your interest and caused you to buy this book but it was not a "planned" visit with specific goals and questions in mind. But now we are ready for **Step Six** on our Purchasing Activity Chart.

In this Chapter of the guide we will try and equip you for your actual "RESEARCH VISITS" — the ones that will begin to accumulate enough data for you to make your final decision down the road.

I have included below some general guidelines as to what you should endeavor to accomplish on your first visit to each site. The **Community Checklist / Profile** in the appendix at the back of the book will be helpful to you in organizing your visits. Prior to venturing out, I would like you to go to the nearest office supply retailer and purchase the following items that will be valuable to you in preserving and reviewing your collected data:

— A fifteen pocket legal size accordion folder
— Legal size manila folders
— Yellow and orange highlighters
— A pack of letter-sized yellow pads
— A few favorite pens
— A small cassette tape recorder
— A 25 foot tape measure
— Plastic marker tabs/labels for the folder

— I also recommend that you purchase a good and convenient sized camera if you don't already have one. Camcorders are good ideas only if you are well experienced and have the stamina to carry it around.

The fifteen pocket folder will be your "bank" of information on the communities you will be visiting. The first thing you are going to do is set up the first file and mark it **OUR OLD HOUSE**. In this file I want you to make a sketch of your current home's floor-plans with room measurements. Go to the library and make six or eight copies for future use. Also include the measurements of your biggest pieces of furniture so that you will be able to make sure they will fit into the new home. Kingsize beds, dining room tables, china closets, corner hutches, and other pieces that you are not going to part with must be measured. And don't forget that double door refrigerator either.

Now that you know your house a little more quantitatively and you have your pen and pad in hand, it's time to make your first visit. Hopefully, you have been collecting data from the newspapers, radio, friends and have at least five or six places to go visit. If you're not at that point yet, then review Chapter Two and get working on those resources on page 32.

One approach I recommend in selecting your first "target" community is to go to one of the ones that you have NOT heard so much about. If you go to the "hottest" place in town, it may be difficult to be objective with your evaluation of some of the smaller communities you will visit. Sizes of front gates, amount of waterfalls and square footage of clubhouses may be impressive but may "blind you" to other more important considerations. Take some time to visit the older communities in your area at the beginning of your research. See how they were constructed ten or fifteen years ago. It will make you appreciate the strides we have made over this explosive growth period.

When you have the first new community picked out, plan a weekday visit if possible (rainy— even better because the salesperson will have more time for you) and proceed as follows:

— Enter the community gates as if you were a visitor and proceed past the sales center. Take a slow drive around the community. Open the windows of your car and take in all that your senses will allow.

Notice: — The condition of the homes
— The variety of model types
— The streets and lighting
— The landscaping on occupied homes
— What are the residents doing?
— Where are the cars parked?
— Are there trucks, boats, sheds?
— Where is the clubhouse?
— Are people using the clubhouse?
— Stop the car and LISTEN
— Are residents waving at you?
— Are the houses close together?
— Are the house colors mixed well?
— How does the grass look? Green?
— Where are the garbage cans?
— Are there any trees in common areas?
— Do any lots look especially good?
— Is there good and clean signage?
— Was there a guard or security car?
— Do you see satellite dishes, awnings?
— Are the home's elevations varied?

Return now to the Sales Center and park.

Upon entering the Sales Center, take notice of how you are greeted. Is it friendly? Is the receptionist smiling? When she presents you with the registration card, fill it out as completely as you can. As you are writing, take in the feeling of the sales center. Are there pleasant voices and happy prospects with sales-people? Does it seem like a friendly place?

She will now do one of several things. Most sales professionals now agree that a quick introduction to the community by the salesperson is the best way to begin your relationship with your possible future builder. If the receptionist just hands you a brochure, you are not getting the maximum amount of informa-tion from your visit. So, in that event, ASK if you can speak to a salesperson first. They will be more than happy to invite you into their office and give you a quick rundown on the community and the models you are about to see. You may even find out something in that first three minutes that eliminates the community from your target list. So don't shortchange yourself. And, don't shortchange the salesperson either. Assuming that he or she is a true professional coun-selor, they will be invaluable to you throughout the purchasing process. So get to know them now and let them know a little about you too.

With the preliminary information known and the model brochure in hand, it's time to go through the models. If this community is like most, there will be a few things in common that you will have to remember.

— Most well designed communities now have a standard product model where you will be able to see the standard grade (not color) of carpeting, padding, vinyl flooring, kitchen cabinets, countertops, lighting, fixtures, and appliances. This makes it much easier when you are trying to predict what your model of choice will cost.

— The models usually are arranged with the smallest first moving up to the largest last. That also corresponds to the pricing levels as well.

— Options and upgrades on most models are not clearly marked. This is primarily because it would look like a used car lot instead of a home if they did. You will have to rely on the salesperson to explain the options to you when you return to his or her office.

— The last model will bring you back through the sales center. This is called a "trap" for obvious reasons. But, actually it is the right place to be because you WILL have questions for your counselor.

— Models may or may not be on standard size lots. You will have to ask the salesperson what the spacing between homes is and what the standard lot sizes are.

On your model walk-through the first time, you should not be focusing on any one particular item but rather should be taking in the entire home "feeling."

If you have five to eleven models to take in, it is pretty obvious that you will have to narrow it down first before you start getting out the tape measure. What you are trying to determine is if you can "picture yourself" in the home. That's all you want to do on this visit. My recommendations to you for your model walk through are listed below:

1. Walk slowly and walk together with your spouse. If you separate, you may miss an important feature for THEM.

2. Look at the overall appearance and condition of the outside of the model. The roof, the siding, the windows, the front door and key lock. Does it look as if it has been kept well and cared for by the builder?

3. Pay attention to the quality detail in the home. The paint job, the drywall work, chair rails, counter-tops, sliding doors and windows. Be critical but understand that thousands of people may have been through the model before you.

4. In each room, stand there and see how it "feels." Am I comfortable here? Is this room too small for its purpose?

5. "Picture" yourself living in the home.

6. Proceed through all of the models in the same manner. Don't look at the price sheet. That is not why we are here today. Today, we just want to see how it "FEELS."

7. When you get to the floorplans that you know make sense for you, you can be more specific in "picturing yourself" living in these homes. Will your fur-

niture fit? Will the grandkids have a room to play in? Can my husband work in the garage and still have his car inside?

8. After the last model has been viewed, and while still in the model area, think back to see which one or two you liked best and mark them on the brochure. Then go back into them and spend a few more minutes thinking about whether or not these could "work" for you and your retirement needs. Think about your furniture again. Will you have to buy new or will most of it fit? Try and picture it.

9. Now return to the Sales Center and wait until your salesperson comes out to get you. If he doesn't and he is free, then get his attention. If he's busy then ask if you can ask a few questions of another salesperson in his absence. This is your time remember and you want to find out more.

"Well what did you think?" — a frequent question of a busy salesperson but one that he actually wants the answer to.

At this point, I hope that you are back in his or her office because you need some key information and it is not available on the sales office floor. You are beginning to accumulate needed information for the Community Profile Sheets in the appendix. That can be filled out at home and not in the busy salesperson's office. But today on visit number one you want to get answers to the following questions IF you like what you have seen in the model center:

FIRST VISIT QUESTIONS

— Can I have an exact list of options in the model that we liked? And what is the cost of the model as it stands?

— Is there a full list of options that we can take home and study?

— What are the standard warranties on the home and its components?

— What is the size of the community and what is the status of homes completed and homes sold?

— Can you tell me a little something about the builder?

— Is there a more complete brochure we may have? And a standard feature list?

— What is your standard build time?

— Do you have sale of home contingencies?

— Which is your most popular model?

— When do you anticipate being sold out?

— When is your next price increase?

— Do you have any purchasing incentives we should know about?

— Where is the nearest shopping mall?

— What are the nearest recreational activities?

— Why do you feel this is the place to buy?

— Where will your next community be built?

— Can you recommend a place for lunch?

— What are your most popular options?

— Can we have a copy of the resident's association newsletter? The public offering statement?

Don't expect them to say yes to the Public Offering Statement. That will be given to you when and if you go to contract on the home. But you may ask them if you can hear about the rules and regulations section of the POS. Maybe they will let you read it in their office. It's worth a try.

When you have received all of your answers and don't have any additional questions, gather up your materials. Later you will place them inside of your first community slot in your accordian folder. If you choose to you may go back outside and snap a picture of the home you really like so it will be fresh in you mind. You can now buy 12 exposure print film which will eliminate confusion and not waste money. Use up all twelve shots on each community and then mark the envelope when you bring it to the drugstore or photo shop.

Go have lunch where the nice salesperson suggested and bring your materials in with you. Review them at lunch so that if you have questions or need to confirm something you can return to check the fact before you drive too far away. That night make notes in the brochure on the models that you are thinking about. Use a yellow highlighter for the things in the brochure that you like and an orange highlighter for the things that you don't like. Do your Community Checklist Profile then go to bed. You've just survived the first of several visits in search of your new home.

Chapter Seven

CAN WE BELIEVE
THE NEW HOME SALES PITCH

Every salesperson gets paid for selling his product to customers like yourselves. Some are better at it then others. Some apply pressure in varying degrees depending on their ability to work with people, their degree of empathy with your particular situation, and the pressures applied to them from their bosses who are the builders and developers of these communities and facilities.

If you are lucky enough to get a salesperson that knows his product and his market and the details of the best ways to counsel you toward your purchase, then you can believe him (or her). But, you are still the one responsible for signing the check. You are still the one responsible for making the right decision. The question should be " Have I done enough research into my purchase of a retirement home to TRUST MYSELF?

I think you will succeed. After all, you have taken a giant step and purchased this book. You are trying to be careful and smart. That should be enough.

I want to share with you some key elements of my sales presentation that I use every day in active adult communities where I have sold many homes over the years.

If I assume that YOU are sitting in front of me at our first visit interview, and after I have determined that you are thinking of moving in the next 12 months or so, I will undoubtedly tell you what your options are regarding a purchase of a home in my community. I will ask you to go through the following checklist which you will often respond to with nods and "*been there- done* that" remarks.

(I will say)— " *In order for you to decide if this move is right for you you must first discuss the following factors between yourselves and agree on the answers. If you're not agreed, then it is likely that no decision will be made and you will not move*":
   First— *Do you* **REALLY** *want to leave where you are now? If you spend twenty thousand dollars on the home, will it be changed enough for you to be happy there? You could avoid all of this moving activity and stay put. It would be a lot easier.*"
   Second— *Have you truly explored the out of state opportunities that might exist? You wouldn't want to move here and then find out that your neighbors from back home had moved to Arizona and are happy as larks because they found the perfect community for a fraction of these prices? Take some trips. Go to North Carolina, Florida, Arizona. Take the time to*

get informed about what else might be out there. Take some weeks or weekend trips and have some fun in the process. You may even find that your kids like the idea.

Third— If you have already decided because of commitments to family or business or culture that you are going to stay in this area then have you investigated all the other senior communities in the surrounding counties. I may even suggest some good competitors to them. Remember, the smarter the customer is the better buyer he will become. And we will all win.

Fourth— If you've fully researched all of your options and you've decided that you are coming to this area, then I think our community is your best choice. And then I explain why.

Throughout my presentation, I am trying to advise my buyers of some very important matters that can help focus their decision to buy.

— Do they know why they are moving?
— Are they aware of out of state opportunities?
— Is their commitment to family strong?
— Do they know the other communities well?
— Are they going to listen to me about here?

I am also trying to establish a trust relationship with them as quickly as possible so that they will begin to believe all details and facts that I will tell them throughout the process. It is a process that begins on the first visit and continues after they move-in. All of my customers are my friends. Before they buy and after. You should seek that kind of a relationship with your community salespeople. If it's missing, tell the sales manager and get another agent.

Another part of my presentation will undoubtedly include my list of comparisons between one community and another. I tell my customers to make sure and consider:
— The traffic congestion at different times of the day and week.
— The maintenance fee amount, structure and the outlook for increases.
— The size of the community. Will they be comfortable there. (Be it too small or too big).
— The perceived quality of the home and the guarantees from the builder.
— The price including options.
— The size and content of the clubhouse as it relates to your specific needs.
— The feeling of the surrounding area.
— Proximity to golf, tennis, beaches and other recreational activities.
— The design of the homes.
— Details of the sale of home contingency.
— The effectiveness and quality of the builder's sales and construction staff.
— The need for a guarded security gate.
— The town's tax structure and outlook.
FACTS— FACTS— FACTS. The more you have to consider, the better your choice will become. And the more you rely on the guidance of your sales person at the new community, the less likely you are to

have problems down the road.

For every community or facility you will now visit, the salesperson or retirement counselor or nursing supervisor will be trying to "sell" you on their location. You will have to become disciplined and organized to separate the fact from the fluff.

As you hear each sales presentation, listen for clues from the salesperson as to how sold THEY are on their community. If they are not excited about their product, then how can you be.

As you visit one community and facility after another, you will soon decide which type will be best for you. Health, age, and financial conditions determine a lot of the choice. When you've got the category picked, then collect all the data and materials that you can to insure that your needs are going to be met.

So — go out now and fill your folder with as many places as you can visit. Use your checklist, your camera, and your imagination. You have the tools and the preparation to get started. And be careful not to see too many places at once. A maximum of two a day is the most I recommend.

In the following two chapters we will reiterate the primary decision factors that you will be using to focus you to a category and then to the ultimate selection of your next home location.

ESTATE PLANNING

COMMUNITY SIZE

KIDS GRANDKIDS

PART-TIME WORK

OUR HEALTH STATUS

HOME DESIGN PRICE

CLUBHOUSE SOCIALIZATION

REAL ESTATE TAXES

AM I TOO OLD

BUY NEW OR RESALE

TOWN LOCATION

DOCTOR BUTCHER BAKER

STAY HERE DON'T MOVE

SECURITY

TYPE OF COMMUNITY

HOME OWNER'S ASSOCIATION

CAN I SELL MY HOUSE

FINANCES MORTGAGES LEGAL

THE EIGHTEEN DECISION FACTORS

Over thousands of interviews and hundreds of home sales, I have identified 18 key purchase factors that are major determinants in the decision to buy a retirement home of any type. Whether you are considering an active adult community or an assisted care facility, the factors are, with minor exception, consistent from one buyer (or couple) to another.

At the core of these decision factors are the primary concern elements of:

HEALTH
FINANCIAL CAPABILITY
CONCERN FOR FAMILY
FEAR OF THE UNFAMILIAR

I will briefly review each of the factors below and try to provide some insight as to their importance to your decision. When you are finished reviewing these decision determinants, I want you to analyze your feelings about each category and try to prioritize in your own mind those that are most important to you and your spouse. As you continue to visit each new community, and as you keep these most important factors in mind, you will begin to consciously narrow your choices down to a select few communities and locations. Then you can prepare to make your more intense re-visits to these top candidates.

DECISION FACTORS

Factor 1. Can we stay where we are?

(Often heard)—"It would be so much easier not to go through all of this research and uncomfortable car travel. If only we could stay in our old house for our golden years."

Nice thought — but usually you're looking at new homes for a reason. Can you relate to these?:

— We need a new roof, furnace, and windows
— Our town is changing for the worse
— We have no more friends living here
— The grass, snow, and yard work is too much
— The kids have all moved to other states
— We can't go up and down stairs anymore
— We never socialize out of the house
— Medical problems require easier living
— I can't clean this big house anymore
— We're "supposed to" retire. Aren't we?
— If we fix it up, we won't recoup our invest
      ment if we decide to sell it later
— The real estate market is great

— We have to dig up an oil tank in the yard
— Our septic system is shot
— We want to be near the shore and golf
— The traffic has become a nightmare
— Our kids want us nearer to them
— We need to get our money out of this house
— We want a simple home to "lock & leave"
— We deserve a new house and clean air

You have your special reasons for wanting to stay. One of the reasons most often thought about but not discussed are the "memories" in the old house developed over years. Your children being born, and growing up. The birthdays and weddings. Decades of great days and nights with family and friends. I have often discussed this with my customers and I have a useful outlook for you to consider.

— The memories that you have enjoyed for years in your old house are IN YOUR HEART and IN YOUR HEAD — they are PORTABLE. They are not attached to the bricks and sheathing of your house. That's the beauty of memories— you CAN take them with you. —

Your other reasons may be strong ones too. But you must remember that life is short and we are only here for a little while. It's just a visit. You have paid your dues and now it's YOUR TIME. And, you really should make the most of it.

Factor 2. What TYPE of facility or community?

We have introduced you to the variety of choices open to you for your "retirement years" residence. They range from the most restrictive nursing home setting where you have little personal freedom to the most independent "spot built" home where you again are in total control of every aspect of home ownership.

In past chapters, we've outlined plenty of guidance on the items that you have to assess to properly identify your needs. You will need to select the right kind of living environment for your current and projected financial and health condition as well as your other more personal criteria.

Couples that appear before me usually haven't taken the time to review the factors I've identified in Chapter Two. They often aren't sure of their health or financial capability. They often have no opinion on whether or not a mortgage would be approved if they applied for one. And in general they are not properly prepared to make their decision to purchase.

Since most of you are very interested in the active adult community segment, let me generally outline the "profile" of a successful candidate for this type of living. Hopefully, it will apply to you and you can focus your attention on this category.

A typical buyer in the newer active adult

communities will generally fit the following description:

  — Age is 50 to 71
  — One or both are in excellent health
  — Current house is paid in full
  — Is receiving pension and S.S. income
  — Is above average in financial strength
  — One will want to do part-time work
  — One wants to do volunteer work
  — Has been moderately social in their lives
  — Wants their independence but knows their
      limitations and need for one-level living
  — One or both wants to get the other spouse
      into a new home and a planned social atmos-
      phere in case something happens to them
  — Loves their kids but has decided that their
      happiness in retirement is important too
  — Makes "a few" good friends relatively easily
  — Wants a home they plan from "scratch"
  — Has a parent that is in need of full time med-
      ical care or is in a nursing home nearby
  — Is ready to spend the next thirty years redis-
      covering the youthful lifestyle they enjoyed
      when they were just starting out.

If you (and your spouse) clearly identify your needs, and do the initial site visits of all types available to you, the selection of the retirement setting that is right for you will become quickly known. Research will pay you HUGE rewards. Do the visits.

Factor 3. The children and those grandkids.

Whether or not children are a help or a hindrance to the purchasing process for your next home, they are certainly a major consideration. After all, you have spent your entire adult life taking care of them and making sure that their decisions were guided by your experienced hand. Why shouldn't they have a say in this next move of yours?

Time and time again, singles or couples come in to see the model homes and then finally say "We're gonna bring the kids back to look next weekend, then we'll make our decision."

Every one of you will have to decide the degree of role your children or grandchildren will play in your purchase of a home and more importantly the choice of location for your retirement residence. Some of you will not buy because your eleven year-old granddaughter says that she will miss you. Others will listen to your sons and daughters tell you that you should economize and come live in an apartment nearer to them. Each of you will have to decide if YOU are the important one or if YOUR SPOUSE is the important one or if, indeed, the KIDS are the important ones. It will be different for everyone.

As for me. I've got three grown sons and have just been blessed with my first grandchild. And, while I am looking forward to all of the grandfather things that will undoubtedly happen over the next twenty-five years, I have already decided that I am not going to revolve my retirement around them. They will have to revolve their timetables and vacations around me and my wife. For when we decide to retire, it will be OUR TIME to enjoy the next "window of living" that we are blessed with.

Factor 4. The doctor, the butcher, and the baker.

You're quite set in your ways where you are right now. You have lived in the same town for thirty-five or more years so why shouldn't you be? You have a great set of doctors that know everything about your health and your peculiarities. You have gone to the same barber or hair stylist for twelve years and NOBODY else will be able to cut YOUR hair. The man next door knows where to get the best tomatoes in Pennsylvania and he goes there every other week-end and brings you back a bag full. Your grocery store is owned by your best friend's husband and he's been doing great against the SUPERSTORES that have sprung up over the last ten years. He expects your weekly visits and depends on your purchases. How will he survive if everyone in the town leaves? The list goes on and on.

My friends, we are all different and we are all the same. Every town has everything that you will ever need. Every town has wonderful store owners, doctors, lawyers, barbers, and dentists. Everyone had to come from somewhere and somewhere is everywhere.

When I recently relocated to southern Ocean County, New Jersey, I was worried about changing dentists. I had been going to the same one for about eight years and was quite happy with his methods, and his personality. The thought of having a NEW person working on my mouth was very stressful.

After getting several recommendations, I took the plunge and made an appointment for a "cleaning" and examination (just to see if I liked the atmosphere in this small town medical office.) I went there at 9:00 A.M. on a Wednesday morning.

I had never been treated so well or so professionally. The teeth cleaning which is always a stressful visit went wonderfully. For the first time in my life, the hygienist asked me if I wanted to have my gums "numbed" before she began. I said yes and she gave me a mild rinse of anesthetic. She then proceeded to "water-jet" clean my teeth. When that was done, she used her more terrorizing tools and scrapped my teeth, one after the other, painlessly. Completing the process with a polishing, I glanced at my watch and noticed that I had been in the chair for ONE HOUR. My previous dentist never spent over twenty minutes on this procedure and never used the techniques that I underwent. And while he used to charge me ninety dollars for the twenty minute process, the new doctor charged me fifty-five for the expanded way. Of course, I love my new dentist and the hygienist and recommend them to everyone. (Oh, incidently, my previous dentist never sent my old ex-rays that I requested).

My point is, folks, that you will survive the new search for services, and stores, and places to go to dinner and to have fun. It's all part of the retirement process. You will find these places with your spouse or with new friends and will enjoy the renewed "spirit" of pioneerism that made this country great.

Also remember that your existing professionals will be able to recommend local professionals located near to where you will moving. So if you need a good cardio-vascular man, you will certainly be able to interview him before you actually make the transition.

Be confident, trust in your own abilities and flexibilities, and be reminded that you are YOU everywhere you go and people will usually react to you in a manner which mirrors how you are treating them.

Factor 5. Community location.

You are going to decide upon a community location with the following considerations in mind:

— Population and "feel" of the town
— Tax rate and degree of planned stability

— Proximity to
    — Shopping and malls
    — "In-walking distance" services / stores
    — Recreational sites (beaches, parks,etc)
    — Hospitals and doctors
    — Major interstate roadways
    — Police, fire, rescue
    — Senior activity centers
    — Public transportation
    — Restaurants
    — Golf courses
    — Airports
    — Other adult communities

— Travel time to location of children
— Traffic patterns and road congestion
— Nature of community (be it rural or city)
— Senior incentives in the town or community
— Character of bordering neighbors of the site
— Town median home price vs. your home
— Access to "walking and biking" trails

You've all known about the real estate importance of LOCATION-LOCATION-LOCATION in selecting a home. The most important consideration is how you feel about the location of your target community in light of how YOU live your lives.

A customer came in to me one day and said that they had their decision narrowed down to two communities. When I asked what had brought them to this point in their search, they remarked that they were absolutely disgusted with the traffic in the particular part of Long Island that they currently lived in. And that even though the two communities they were considering were a bit remote from the main town and services, that they liked it that way. They wanted to have a carefree lifestyle — but AWAY from the maddening crowd. For them it was the primary consideration after the quality and price of the home.

Whatever your particular needs relative to community location, don't let another 30 minute drive stop you from buying somewhere you really like. You are WORTH another 30 minutes for the kids to drive. Please know that (and get a little more selfish).

Factor 6. The size of the community.

"Different things for different people." "One man's dream is another's nightmare." "Too big". "Too small". "Not enough activity". "Too much activity". "Nowhere to hide". "Too many things to do". " Looks like an institution." "Looks just too small and remote." "Too massive — We'll be lost in there." —Size directly relates to the feeling of comfort and security that you will enjoy in your new home.

Since many of the active adult shoppers like yourselves are in the 55 to 65 age category, we find that you are giving more serious consideration to the SIZE of the community that you choose than would say a 70 to 80 year-old buyer. This is predominantly due to the fact that the older you get, the more time of your day is spent IN the home rather than out of it. Therefore, your satisfaction with the interior design and quality of your house takes precedence over how many neighbors you have on the outside and how close their properties may be to your own.

When "younger" buyers of 50 to 55 come in to look at new adult communities, among the biggest complaints are usually:

- **The houses are too close together**
- **There are just too many homes here**
- **They all look alike**
- **You can see in all of the windows**
- **There's NO privacy**
- **That clubhouse pool is TOO small**
- **What happened to all of the trees**

These and other negative comments relate to the size of the community as designed by the developer and/or builder.   They are more psychological concerns than ones that are peculiar to number of homes. They are really saying that they are not yet ready for the lifestyle of an adult community. They are not yet at a point in their lives when the "trade-offs" of loss of privacy and loss of individuality for comfort, convenience, socialization, and security are worth the associated benefits.   They still want large lots, custom designs, bigness of floorplans, and personal outdoor items like pools, hot tubs, and their own well for drinking and irrigation water.

But you are over 55. And since you will be encountering communities from 200 units to some of over 2000, you must discuss your personal feelings about community size before you set about researching locations.

Underlying the size of the community and its' feeling of "bigness" or "smallness" will be the ability of the developer to create a certain attractive "ambiance" with the land parcel that is available to him for the project. This will always relate to the costs involved, the financial ability of the developer, and the sale price of the homes. Large communities with plenty of houses packed closely together and a minimum of trees and landscaping will have lower than average prices. And that is necessary for some buyers. Small, elaborate, "upscale" adult communities with large lots, plenty of trees, and more amenities than the bigger communities will certainly have to cost more per home. But, again, for some it will be worth the extra expense.

Large, elaborate, and exclusive adult communities with a multitude of available options that can bring home prices over the $ 200,000 range have to be examined based upon where they are located and their comparison to surrounding average home prices in the resale market. For, if you build a "shangra-la" in the middle of the desert , it may be out of place and may not attract the expected buyers due to the incongruence with the neighboring population.

For active adults seeking their perfect retirement home or community, size does very certainly play a large role. As one of the eighteen factors being identified in this chapter, its importance to you can only be decided after seeing the degree of ingenuity, design, and good taste created at the community by the builder that is trying to make you a buyer.

Factor 7. Clubhouses, Recreation, and Amenities

All new active adult communities will have a clubhouse of some sort for use by the residents at the community. Generally it will include at the minimum:

— A "great room" for parties and dances
— Kitchen with minimal appliances
— Physical fitness room with equipment
— Arts and crafts room
— Library
— Card room or card area
— Pool table or two
— Outdoor pool
— Shuffleboard, bocce, horse shoes
— Men's and Women's changing rooms /baths
— Small office and storage area
— Outdoor seating area around pool
— Locked door with security code for residents

— Walking trail
— Community flower garden
— Community vegetable garden

More elaborate additions might include:

— Indoor pool
— Saunas, hot tubs, whirlpools
— Stock Market "ticker tape" rooms
— Greenhouses
— Men's and Ladies' separate facilities
— Restaurant / Grill
— Beverage service
— Full-time Recreation Director
— Tennis courts
— Lighted night activities
— Paddle tennis
— Putting greens
— Executive golf course
— Regulation golf course
— Paved bike trails
— Paved running trails
— Private rooms for meetings / rentals
— Pool snack bar with beverage service
— Dedicated aerobics room
— Nurse / Doctor station / Infirmary
— Waterfalls, ponds and fountains

It seems with every new community comes a new innovation to the clubhouse design or contents that is endeavoring to make an impact on potential

buyers. Some have even abandoned the term clubhouse and called the new edifices of twenty thousand
or more square feet "Spas", Fitness Centers or
Lifestyle Resorts. Where will it all end?

Money is where it all ends.

The more elaborate the clubhouse design the
higher the cost of the home you are going to buy. The
more intense the package of amenities that are offered
within, the higher the monthly maintenance fees will
be that you have to pay. It is simple, yet very complex.

Most 55 year-old buyers DON'T YET KNOW
how important the clubhouse design will be for them
in their style of retirement. Will they use the pool?
Will they work out on the fitness equipment? Will
they really spend any time in the " stock market
room?" These and other questions can only be
guessed at by the prospective buyer. But, guess you
must — because you will be dazzled by the size of
some of these complexes. And you will be wondering
if you are retiring or going to the Catskills for an all-
inclusive make-over.

I'm not going to keep you dangling on this decision. I have some very specific feelings and recommendations for you to examine and think about. It all
goes back to identifying your needs — your REAL
needs. You know YOU the best. And your spouse
should be learning to know YOUR needs by now too.

In evaluating "What" you need in a clubhouse and associated amenities, review the following concepts then make your decision as to the importance of the size and content of the clubhouse and recreation components of the communities you have visited:

1. What sports or activities do I enjoy NOW?
2. Talk to your significant other about their's.
3. Do I need a large clubhouse with 24/7 activities in order to "socialize" or can I meet people on my own?
4. Would I be willing to join a golf or swim club nearby to enjoy recreational facilities if they were not available at my community?
5. Do I want the services of a recreation director to "plan out" MY recreational week?
6. Is my health such that I need a full service clubhouse with "one-stop" recreational shopping?
7. Am I willing to pay $ 70-120 or more monthly for an impressive clubhouse?
8. Will I be bringing a lot of guests there?
9. What will I miss most if it's not there?
10. Am I going to join a lot of committees?
11. Do I want the clubhouse more for my spouse than I do for myself?

If you review the answers to these questions honestly, you will be able to prioritize the importance of the size of the clubhouse and amount of amenities for you and your spouse. This factor is **very** important.

Factor 8. Homeowner's Associations / fees.

Every community or residential complex that is fee simple or condo ownership which has common areas or a clubhouse will undoubtedly have a homeowner's association for the management of the common elements. Common elements usually mean open space grass areas, the clubhouse facility and the surrounding ground area, community irrigation systems, drainage mechanisms, perhaps roads if they are "privatized" by the community, landscaped entrances to the facility, and any other part of the complex that inures to the benefit of the resident population as a whole.

The Homeowner's Association or HOA as it is frequently referred to is initially comprised of representatives of the builder and several elected residents who choose to serve as trustees. After a certain percentage of homes are owner occupied, the residents will fully control the management of the organization and be responsible for the financial viability of the entity. Voting takes place on all issues with each home in the community having a vote. All the details of the HOA are usually contained in the community's Public Offering Statement which is usually given to buyers when they execute an Agreement of Sale with the builder / developer.

Prospective buyers should know that a community with an HOA has some important differences than a regular home purchase where there is NO association to deal with and should fully understand these differences and characteristics before placing a reservation deposit at a new community.

As I stated earlier in the book, your real estate attorney should be consulted if you have any questions on the Homeowner's Association, the Public Offering Statement, or any other legal item pertaining to your new home purchase.

In general, following are some facts about HOA's that are important for you to know:

— There are always Rules and Regulations associated with communities with common elements. You must be familiar with them before you are out of the attorney review process (after Agreement of Sale) (Legal process will be covered in Chapter Twelve)

— The management of the HOA is made up of elected homeowner trustees. The number of trustees increases as the number of homes occupied rises.

— The builder may or may not be subsidizing the expenses of the HOA prior to resident control.

— Fees for HOA's may rise to meet the actual expenses of the community at the discretion of the HOA management and voting homeowners.

— Typically, the builder will guide the home-owner's through a long and comprehensive "transition" period before they take over control completely. This insures that the homeowners will stand a better than average chance of meeting with management success in their required activities.

— HOA's rely on volunteerism from the residents if the budget is to be maximized. All are encouraged to participate in the numerous committees that will be formed.

— Typical committees of an HOA may be:

> Covenants Committee - Oversees Bylaws
> Social Committee
> Landscape Committee
> Sunshine Committee
> Financial Committee
> Clubhouse Operations
> Pool Committee
> Sports and Competition Committee
> Publicity Committee
> Management Committee
> Legal Matters Committee
> Community Relations Committee
> Builder Liaison Committee
> Special Events Committee

— HOA's are separate legal entities with their own financial reporting requirements to IRS.

— HOA's are meant to be a tool for the residents to BETTER enjoy their community and are not meant to be a political machine or a police mechanism to restrict people's rights.

— HOA's will be more successful and run more efficiently if the community residents PARTICIPATE as well as make suggestions.

The biggest fear of new home purchasers who are not familiar with HOA's is the degree of "control" the Association will have over their individuality in making their home personalized. For example, "Will I be able to fly "Old Glory" in the front yard? Will I be restricted on making additions and alterations to the outside of my home? Can I put a wooden cow in my front shrub bed? Are satellite dishes allowed? Where can I put my trash can? etc.

The second biggest fear is often related to the visits of grandchildren. There are many stories circulating about unfare rules in this regard. Will I be restricted in the number of days my grandkids can visit? When will they be able to use the pool? Can they live with me if something happens to my kids?

MY suggestion is for you to become familiar with the rules and regulations BEFORE you buy. Tell your salesperson that you want to review the rules and regulations in his office, while he watches if he likes. Even though you do not see the Public Offering

Statement and the Rules and Regulations until
"Contract" day, there is no reason why you can't get a
sneak preview before that. Ask. I think you'll succeed.

Remember, the HOA is made up of RESI-
DENTS just like yourself. They are trying to keep the
community consistent in appearance and smooth running. Don't be afraid of the HOA — rather embrace it
as an ally helping your home and community to
become more attractive.

Factor 9. Security considerations

Last week, I heard about a gated community of
1500 houses that had twelve cars broken into by van-
dals. They were parked on the street and IN drive-
ways. I did say the community was GATED didn't I?

I'm of the opinion that if a burglar wants to get
into your home, he will. They never have had I.Q.
tests for these morons, so why should we think that a
guard house or a roving security car would have any
impact on their decision to randomly pick a house to
enter?

When evaluating security considerations at a
retirement complex, we must understand that different
people will have different experiences throughout life
and may need a wide variety of assurances as to their
apparent or real safety. If for example, you were a city

dweller and had your house broken into in the past, then you might be more likely to be security conscious than if you lived on a farm on the plains and never had the need to lock your doors.

Aside from the extra monthly costs, the security considerations in your new community and new home are:

— Must I have a staffed guardhouse up front?

— Will an alarm system on my home be sufficient to make me feel confident in my safety?

— What is the crime rate in THIS town?

— Where is the police station?

— Are these public or private streets?

— Is the main street a thoroughfare?

— Will we be home most of the time or do we take frequent one and two day trips?

— Are my neighbors home (to watch) most of the time?

— Will the "Big Brother" image of the guardhouse bother me or offend my guests?

— Is there a 24 hour patrolled service on site?

— Is "Enhanced" 911 in the town?

— Are there "panic button" services available?

— What has been the history in the community so far?

The need for safety and security in a new home is very personal. Think about what you and your spouse really NEED. Do what feels comfortable without being embarrassed or too proud to admit you fears.

Factor 10. The Home Quality, Design,—Price

— and ALL THOSE OPTIONS

This is by far the biggest and most important factor for you to consider in making your decision to purchase. Where should we start? What is the most important aspect of the house that you should be concerned with? How can I tell one builder's quality apart from another's? The answer is simple. We have been getting you ready for the last seven chapters. You must research — and then do more research. You can't possibly learn too much about the builder, his methods of construction, his warranties, his vendors, the price and qualities of his energy and interior design options and the myriad of other items relating to your next (best) home.

Quality

An analysis of the home quality MUST start with an analysis of the builder. Consider conducting the following activities:

1. Find out other communities he has built and visit them. Talk to residents there if possible.
2. Call up the township building department or planning officer and ask their opinion on the construction quality of the homes or the competence of the builder.

3. Ask for and call the builder's financial institution (if they don't have a public company or an annual report). Ask about the financial strength of the builder.

4. Get accurate details about how many homes the builder has delivered over the past five years.

5. Ask about the standard warranties on the home. Ask about "special warranties" of this builder.

6. Make sure the 10 or 15 year warranties are with reputable companies.

7. Ask for the manufacturer's names of the home construction materials and option components. Are they buying first line materials or second quality goods?

8. Ask your salesperson about the builder. How is he to work for?

9. How long does it take to build a home?

10. Have the closing dates been met on the homes already occupied at the community?

11. What and where is the next community to be built by this builder?

12. Are there other communities being built in other locations at this time?

13. Call the Chamber of Commerce and Better Business Bureau to review existing or past complaints against this builder.

14. Ask residents on the street at the community for their opinion on the quality and reputation of the builder. Don't forget to ask them if they are happy there too.

15. Ask when you can MEET THE BUILDER.
16. Ask if they ever have construction tours with the builder. Can you have a special one?
17. Ask what construction methods exceed the required code requirements. Check with the town.

Once you have a good feeling about the quality of the builder, you can get into house quality by visiting the models, going to see the homes that are under construction in the community, setting up "command performance" visits with the construction department to review their construction methods, and asking the salesperson for the vendor and material information just mentioned. Look at the quality of the 2x4 studs in the homes and the type of roofing and sheathing materials being used. Also be very cognizant of cleanliness on the job site. Are there a lot of cans and bottles left in the houses? Are the houses under construction "broom" clean and ready for the next trade that is coming in? This is always an important signal about the "quality attitude" that you will require when they build your home.

Design

"If you don't like the way they look, you won't be buying anything."

The architects and designers of today are endeavoring to come up with home styles and designs that will suit the broad range of active adults over 55 years of age. The difficulty is that the profiles of these buyers are so varied that coming up with a "perfect model" has been impossible to date. The architect has to try and please:

— Single buyers
— Married buyers
— "Snow birds"
— Grandparents
— Fixed income purchasers
— Wealthy purchasers
— Physically challenged
— Young "Active Adults"
— Low activity homebound buyers
— Those that cook and those that eat out
— Those with big families / Those with none
— Two / One / or No car couples
— Those with hobbies / Those with none

What usually happens is that several model designs are included in the model centers and the buyer then goes from one to another much like the fairy tale character until one feels "just right."

If there are only five or six to look at, that usually can be dealt with easily. But, I have seen model centers with up to fifteen designs and after a while, they all seem to look alike. What is the buyer to do except maybe leave and go get some lunch?

And, while the preference of most buyers would be to see plainly decorated homes with few options, the builder's interior designers often get carried away and "load the homes up" with structural and accessory options that make the price "as-is" way over what the average buyer can afford.

I recommend that when you go through models at new home communities, you follow my procedure in Chapter Six, Where Do We Start?

Along with that, when you're trying to decide on a design that suits your way of living, keep in mind the following:

— You won't be needing all the clothes and furnishings from your old house. This is the time to scale down and live easy — so SCALE DOWN.

— You don't need to impress anybody anymore. This house has to please YOU. Don't buy square footage if you don't need it. This house is supposed to be simple so you can lock it up and head to the Bahamas.

— Find the room that you will enjoy spending 80% of your waking hours in and buy THAT house.

— Don't plan for enough space for ALL of the kids to stay overnight. They will probably NEVER be there at the same time.

— Practice living there. Take fifteen minutes on your second or third visit and MAKE BELIEVE you're planning a weekend party. This role-playing may convince you if the house is right or not for your way of living.

— Think about cleaning it. Don't buy a home that looks good but that will give you headaches later. Cathedral ceilings look great. But how do you get that spider web out of the corner?

— Bring the kids. They can add real insight and confidence to your choice of homes. Let's face it — you want them to be behind you on this move. So, if they are supportive, let them "help" you decide.

— Make sure it is REALLY maintenance-free. Find out how to change furnace filters. What has to be done to the outside of the house and who is responsible to do it?

— When you're placing or rather "trying to place" your old furniture in the new house, consider the possibility of keeping only the very few pieces that you can't part with and buying new for the rest of the home. It will be easier, believe me.

— Make sure you know what structural options are in the home and what the BASE house looks like. Don't be mislead by beautiful entertainment centers or fireplaces that don't come with the home. Study the floorplans and standard features sheet carefully. Also ask your salesperson to go out into the models with you if you are unsure as to what's optional and what's included.

In summary, the design has to appeal to you, has to satisfy your needs for living, playing, and storage space and has to hit the price range that you can afford.

I'm of the opinion that simpler is better this time around. But, you can make this home anyway you want it. After all, you have plenty of time to plan it out.

Price Including Options

How much is this place going to cost me?

In order to determine the final price that your home will cost, you must segregate out the items that contribute to the total. Then you must evaluate them as they relate to your own particular needs. The following list includes most of the cost (price) factors that you will be concerned with in your new home purchase: (Don't forget to deduct builder incentives.)

— The base price of the model you choose
— The extra charge for modified elevations
— Structural options you may add such as
    — sunrooms, screened porches, patios
— Custom structural changes
— Lot premiums (location or size)
— Option packages or deluxe exteriors
— Individual options you want to add
— Upgrades you choose to make
— Addition of basements or crawl spaces
— Interior design options if offered
— Window treatments you will require

Other than actual house and construction costs you will also want to know how much you will be spending on:

— Legal closing costs you will incur
— Mortgage charges you may incur
— Cost of moving from your old house
— Cost of interim housing if needed
— Cost of getting your old home ready for sale
— Cost of selling your house for less if needed
— Real estate commissions, legal expenses

We will cover some of these legal and financial matters a little later. Just understand that there is a lot more to your "real" home price than what is shown on the builder's price sheet. But, let's examine just the house for the moment and review some of the apparent cost items mentioned above.

1. Base Price

The base price of the home shown on the builder's price sheet is the price of the plain model with all of its standard features and no options. You must determine what is included in the home as standard. Most builders will have a standard features sheet which will outline in detail what is included in the base price of the home. Some newer builders are now including a "standard product" model in their sales centers which feature the standard quality of carpet, vinyl, cabinets, lighting, windows, countertops, bathroom components, interior finishes, and appliances. These products WITH a color choice are what you would be provided with in your particular model.

If there is not a standard model, make sure that you scrutinize the standard feature list to make sure you are getting what you expect without paying extra. Such things as garage door openers, garage attic stairs, air conditioning, drawers in bathroom vanities, knobs on the kitchen cabinets, decorator light switch plates, lighting fixtures in kitchens and dining rooms, landscaping and other items that you may ASSUME are standard because they are in the model may cost you extra dollars and extra aggravation when it comes time to "select" your colors and options. Ask questions and get your salesperson into the model to show you what comes with the house and what does not.

Another area of confusion can occur because the builder's interior designer has included "treatments" to vignette the home for better "presentation" to the buying public. For example they may put real wood planking around the perimeter of a room and carpeting in the center. It may look great but not be available in this "split" arrangement. Or they may add a window or a skylight or an expensive ceiling light that "makes the room" but may not be available to you even on an optional basis. Ask the salesperson.

You deserve to know EXACTLY what is standard in the home. And you should also be able to look at the standard colors of these materials and products without a great deal of difficulty. ASK YOUR SALESPERSON. That is their job.

2. Architectural Elevation Upgrades

Sometimes there is a choice of front elevation appearance that gives you a chance to make your home a little more individual in nature. It may be the addition of a different roofline design, some brick or stone to the front of the house, a covered front porch, or a different garage door design that makes your home different from your next door neighbor. The floorplan of the home usually is not affected by your decision on this choice. But the amount of attic storage may be different if the roofline is changed. So take a walk upstairs and take a peek.

3. Structural Options

A considerable profit component for the builder is additional structural options that you may desire to add to the the basic floorplan of your home. Your choice of a large sunroom or a special expanded breakfast area means extra money for the builder. But many feel that it is worth it to make their home more livable and more in tune with their lifestyle needs.

If you choose not to buy these expensive options, don't be so sure that you can add them easily after you move in. Usually, because of the need to submit plans to the Homeowner's Association and the township, and because you will be dealing with a new contractor that is building ONE unit instead of many, you will probably pay more than the original price.

4. Custom Structural Changes

If your builder will allow custom changes to his standard layouts to make the house "just perfect" for you and your furniture, be prepared to pay handsomely for this luxury. The cost of adding a knee-high wall or a door to a living room may not be too bad. But ask for larger room dimensions, moved heating vents, different styles of ceilings, custom bathrooms, fireplaces in non-standard locations, deeper closets, or a different size of garage attic stairs and you're sure to see sticker shock.

Understand that it's not that builders don't want to accommodate your wish. It is simply impractical for them to do so. They are trying to provide you with a home price that is reasonable and to do that they must "standardize" as much as possible. When they "order" a house after your selection process, they prepare purchase orders that are standardized for your particular model. They order from each vendor again and again and it is very confusing when there is a "special" requirement which varies from the norm. And, if they need to make a change after you have made selections, you will most likely incur a sizeable charge if it is not caused by their error.

5. Lot Premiums

In most adult communities today, standard lot sizes are typically 50 x 100 and for most of us this is adequate. Most planned unit developments, however, strive to maximize the profits from the available land and lay out the home sites in a fashion that may make some of them a bit more "premium" than others. This often also takes advantage of a particular feature of the community like an attractive retention basin, a golf course, or a heavily wooded perimeter area. Larger lot sizes, lots bordering open space, lots with green acres backyards, and corner lots are also frequently included in these more expensive home parcels.

Depending on the community and its location, typical lot premiums can range from $500 to $ 50,000 and usually are price determined after the demand for the homes and the community has been confirmed. In other words, the exact premiums may not be known initially at the beginning of a project but rather are set after a track record of sales has been established.

Buyers typically do not like the concept of lot premiums. They would rather ALL lots be the same price even if it meant a higher price for the home. But, the method of setting some lots above the rest in order to garner extra dollars of profit will probably continue forever since there is always a market for these "extra value" locations.

6. Option Packages

Some builders today are endeavoring to simplify the options selection process and are "pre-selecting" option packages for the buyer. They may assemble a grouping of options and assign different names to them such as the "Estate", "Monte Carlo", "Dynasty" or "Falconcrest" collections. Then they add that name to the base model name and come up with the "*Monte Carlo* **Devon**" or the "*Dynasty* **Whittingham**" and so on. Typically the packages can add ten, twenty or even forty thousand dollars to the home price in no time. And, often the buyer will add even more options on top of the package which makes the builder even happier.

7. Options A La Carte

The most frequently used method of ordering options for new homes is to set up appointments with in-house, and on-site interior design specialists who will review the entire list of options with the buyer and write up the order at the same time they do all of the color selections for the standard products and materials. This procedure can be a source of tremendous trepidation to the buyer and because of this, it is recommended that a good deal of time be spent in the "selection room" or "design center" prior to the actual day of ordering. The most important and time consuming process will be color and design selection of carpet, cabinets, vinyl flooring, and countertops for the kitchen and bathrooms. So time should be spent on those items especially. If the model center has been set up with a "standard" house with standard quality of materials, the process will be a little simpler but still time consuming.

Typically, on the day of ordering, you will first meet with the design coordinator in your model of choice. There, you will set about looking at the ceiling fan and electric outlet locations and may also determine where cable connections will be placed. The recessed light locations may also be measured and recorded if you are ordering them for your new home.

The process will then proceed with questions and answers about the specific design of the house and any structural changes you may be asking for. These can be reviewed and presented to the builder for his agreement to build or refusal to accommodate your wishes. But you should know these answers within a few days. (Don't let it go past that.)

When you are finished in the model, you will likely then go to the design center and set about picking out all of the colors and options that will make your house unique to your needs.

The following list of options is a general list of what you will be choosing from at the "selections" appointment. If you are a typical buyer, you will be spending about three hours with the design coordinator choosing:

— Structural options such as dens, expanded garages, extended breakfast areas, sunrooms, screened porches, patios, and decks.

— Products, designs and colors for all flooring zones in the home. These choices will include wood flooring, ceramic floor tile, under padding, carpeting, vinyl flooring, indoor outdoor/carpeting and any custom flooring treatments that you desire and that the builder is willing to accommodate.

— Appliances (styles, upgrades, colors)
— Fireplaces and accessories
— Kitchen and bath countertops
— Exterior house, roof, shutter colors
— Bathroom product options
— Energy saving options
— Kitchen and bathroom cabinets
— Lighting products
— Interior painting or papering options (if offered)
— Plumbing options like hot water heat, special laundry tubs or upgraded water heaters
— Other offered items that you have seen in the model homes, such as entertainment centers, skylights, custom exterior treatments, and mailbox designs, if available.

Buyers today have serious decisions to make as to WHEN they add options to their homes. Of course, the builder would like you to add everything right away so that he receives the maximum sale price for the home. But there are some cases where you may want to wait to add your options at your own pace. I will outline three below for your consideration:

A. *Snowbirds*

If you are only going to be in the home for six months out of every twelve, you may want to consider NOT adding a host of upgrades at this time. Make the house as comfortable as you like but understand that your wear and tear on the home may be minimal. You may not want to "deluxe-outfit" the place since you also will be paying for a second location elsewhere.

B. *Early Retirees*

If you're purchasing now for a retirement three years away, you may want to take it easy on options when the home is initially built since you will probably "re-fit" it later when you go to full time retirement. If you adopt this policy, you might even consider leasing your retirement home to another senior couple until you are ready to occupy it later. You would have locked in the price and location, received rental income to use toward your retirement, and perhaps locked in a low mortgage rate to further enhance the justification for the purchase. If you put in the standard products and only the structural options you desire, you will be able to refresh your home later with new interior treatments exactly as you desire when you are ready to occupy.

C. *Restricted Financial Buyers*

For those on tighter budgets, understand that you can purchase the basic home now and upgrade as your income will allow. The main concern is "getting you" to the active adult lifestyle you seek. The home, in its standard form, still makes you a member of the community. You don't need to follow the Jones' anymore. Buy it simple — then fix it up your way when you can. No one will mind.

In summary, the question of OPTIONS is a personal decision that you and your spouse have to make. I sometimes call it a "shopping excursion". You may choose to shop or not as you see fit and as it relates to your own desires and NEEDS. Be careful, order what is necessary and desired. In other words— shop with your head and not over it.

8. Upgrading

Standard available products in the homes can be upgraded just as specific options can be ordered. Your decision to upgrade is dependent on the same needs and desires you have been using as measuring sticks throughout the options purchasing procedure.

If you have to upgrade to achieve the desired level of comfort or convenience for your lifestyle —then do it. If not — don't.

As an example. Let's say you've always had the top of the line self-cleaning oven and sealed top burner stove all of your working life. When you look at the open burner, less fancy, self-cleaning oven being offered as standard by the builder, your immediate reaction is to get ready for an upgrade. BUT — you're forgetting that you will probably not be cooking as much when you make the transition to retirement. You'll be out to restaurants with friends, you'll be taking more trips out of state or out of the country. The foods you do make will be simpler like chicken and fish. The kids won't be coming over for dinner as much. And, in general, your entire cooking life will be changing. So think it over before you upgrade. You may find that the standard stove will do just fine. (So too may the standard size washer,dryer and dishwasher).

9. Basements / Crawl spaces

Like the structural options that we have mentioned, the addition of a basement or a crawlspace to a home can add considerable cost and may or may not be worth the expense depending on the NEEDS of the buyer.

The most frequently heard reasons for wanting crawl spaces and basements are respectively as follows:

Slab construction is too hard on the feet
Slab construction is too cold
We'll get bugs if we don't have a crawlspace
Repairs may mean we have to "break" the slab
We need a basement for more storage space
We have hobbies that require more square feet
We need a place for a third bedroom or office

Normally, I use the following responses to the above mentioned "reasons" for not having a slab.

Proper, modern slab construction has overcome many of the objections that used to be common with earlier designed cement slabs. More modern materials and procedures and the use of two and three block high cement block foundations with improved moisture and pest barriers have eliminated the negatives almost completely. Today, the term "filled" crawl space might be a more correct term. And, in the case of having to penetrate the slab to make repairs to piping underneath, the patching methods today are far superior to the ones of days past. You are unlikely to see any ill effects of having to "crack" a slab to get to defective piping today.

Regarding coldness of slab construction. The wide number of options of carpet under padding has reduced this objection considerably. And, most seniors don't walk around barefoot anymore either.

The importance of footfall impact today is reduced because most seniors are not walking with the same degree of bounce as they once did. It is not proper sales procedure to tell customers this, but they are really walking softer or "shuffling" a bit more than they did twenty years ago.

Be flexible on this issue, and walk the models to see how they "feel" to you. It really is not the problem that it was in the fifties and sixties when construction techniques were less sophisticated.

Basements and for that matter attics are only asked for by buyers that have not yet fully committed themselves to a reduced complexity in their retirement lives. They indeed, may not be quite ready to enter an active adult community at all.

If a third or fourth bedroom is needed "in case" children may visit or if an office is required because you "might" work a bit longer, these are signals to re-evaluate your needs and readiness for retirement community living. I consider these questions a "red flag" and I usually find that the buyer who asks for these extra square footage add-ons does not ultimately buy in an adult community but may stay in their existing house or build in an all-age neighborhood.

10. Interior Design / Window Treatments

After you close title and move-in, there will still be considerable costs ahead of you in order to make the home exactly the way you want it for your new lifestyle. Plan to research local sources for window treatments, wallpaper, painting contractors, furniture, home furnishings, lighting, home improvement, and storage. You will undoubtedly become a valued customer to many of the local businesses. We will cover this in Chapter Nine, but start to do your research of these local establishments early. It may save you hundreds of dollars or MORE later on.

Factor 11. Job Market — Will I be working?

The next of our eighteen purchasing factors is one that is more of a consideration today than it was to the previous generation. Unfortunately, the baby boomers will have to work much longer than our fathers and mothers did if we are to maintain our standards of living. It has been recently reported that children born after 1946 will ALWAYS be working at least part-time. This is because of probable pending failures in the social security system, unrestrained national government spending, increased taxes and cost of living, and the fact that we are living much longer than we would have ever anticipated.

I have a good friend that I used to play golf with about once a week. One day he was candidly talking to me about his retirement, his health condition, and his finances. It seems that twelve years ago, Jim had a serious heart attack that required him to undergo a quadruple bypass operation. The operation was successful, but he was so shaken and so uncertain about how many years he had left on this earth, that he took early retirement with reduced pension and decided to slow down.

Now at age sixty-nine, Jim is doing fine. But, his remark to me one day on the golf course will never leave my mind. He said. "Jared, I should have died four years ago.— That's when my money ran out." At sixty-nine, Jim is now working at a large home renovation store in the paint department. Not by choice, but out of necessity.

Your decision to work part-time or full-time after you retire will hopefully be more out of desire than from need. But either reason must be considered before you buy this next home. If you decide you want to work twenty hours a week in a major shopping center store, you have to make sure that they will be hiring when you move into the area. Go check it out. Ask them if they hire retired part-time help. Very often, they will appreciate the opportunity to get a seasoned salesperson who actually knows FROM EXPERIENCE how the products are to be used.

Volunteering is a good way to work and make some extra income after you move. Check into the area hospitals and nursing homes. They are always looking for experienced caregivers and aides.

If you have a special hobby or interest, you should investigate the possibility of turning that into a business. If you love to paint, or were an accountant, or like to work in the garden, or work with cars, there may be employers that can utilize your talents for the benefit of their customers. You'll be doing what you love and get paid in the process. Is there something you've always thought you'd be good at? Real estate sales, cutting hair, driving a bus, working with under-privileged kids, or working as a librarian. This may be the time to go for it. But, do it on your terms and with your time schedule. You're retired now— remember ? Investigate. And talk it over with your spouse too. Remember, it's their retirement too. Don't get so caught up again that your health or private life suffers. Discuss it first.

Factor 12. Resale Market forecast.

We will discuss the sale of your house in great detail in Chapter Twelve. The concern for resale mar-ket conditions here as one of the purchase factors is relating to specific conditions at the time you intend to put your old house on the market. Is it the right time to sell or should you wait?

In 1988 we ended a very bright time in the national real estate markets. Homes were selling for very high prices. It was a great time to SELL. It certainly was not the best time to BUY. At the time of printing of this guide, the market is again very good. Most agree it's the best it has been in some twelve years. House prices are firm and rising. Mortgage rates are low. Buyers are anxious and sellers are ecstatic because their homes are selling quickly for the prices they want. It is again a good time to sell. But, will it last? We don't know.

If you are close to retirement, the real estate resale market conditions MUST play a role in moving you to action. You must consider "striking" while the iron is hot. Conversely, should you NOT ACT if the market is bad? Not necessarily. But each seller must make up his mind based upon his needs, his special set of conditions and circumstances that has brought him to this point in time. You must at a minimum seek counsel from someone who knows the realty market well so that you will be properly informed as to the exact conditions and how it might affect the sale of your specific home. So talk to realtors and talk to your accountant. Analyze your finances to determine how much you must make on the sale of your home to make the transition to the new community. If it turns out that you can get to the new home by accepting an offer that is four or five thousand dollars off of your "ideal" selling price, it may be worth the loss in revenue to get on with your move. That four or five thousand dollars is not enough for you to hold up your plan to get to that new lifestyle as soon as possible.

Factor 13. Health Considerations

You know about this factor already. In our chapter on needs, we covered the requirement to assess your physical condition and make some real decisions about what type of facility you need for your golden years. We need only to remind you that this assessment is the most critical factor whether you decide to move or stay in your present house. Take care of yourselves.

I'd like to say a word about moving as it relates to your health. There are pros and cons to this question for you to discuss with your spouse.

— Moving is very stressful and can be physically exhausting if you are not in the best of physical shape.

— The psychological benefit of moving to a new location away from the problems of the old location CAN outweigh the pain of the moving experience.

— You must decide to take a slow route to the move. If an activity took you only one day to do ten years ago — take two days today.

— Farm out the work. Have your kids help with the packing. Also make sure that they take their stuff to THEIR houses. You don't want to move their dead storage or furniture to your new home.

— If you find yourself getting unusual symptoms while you're thinking about moving, you may be stressing yourself out prematurely. Talk to your spouse and your doctor and get it sorted out NOW before you buy this next home.

Factor 14. Should I buy a resale home?

New or resale is always a question for today's senior buyer. And, like most decisions, there is no one right answer for every buyer.

Following are some general advantages and disadvantages of buying a resale home:

Advantages of a Resale home
— Already built — no waiting for construction
— All the "kinks" are out of the house
— No area construction around the house
— Options will cost less than if bought new
— Painted and wallpapered already
— Lawn and landscaping in place
— Usually lower price than new home
— Taxes are absolutely known

Disadvantages of a Resale home
— Can't have house "exactly" as you want it
— Appliance warranties are probably expired
— No guarantees on major house elements
— Usually less "bright" and less storage
— No bug infestation warranties
— No builder or 10 year homeowner warranty
— A lot of cleaning and freshening up expense
— Minor repairs and alterations needed
— No "new" home or community excitement

Factor 15. Estate Planning Implications

What on earth does my estate planning have to do with the purchase of a new home in an adult community?

As we have seen in this chapter, the costs incurred in the purchase of a home are made up of a variety of factors. From the home model we pick to the type of drapes that we buy for the living room windows, every aspect takes its' toll on our pocketbook.

How you structure your purchase in regard to your estate also affects your pocketbook. This factor must be evaluated by the "triumvirate" of YOU, your ACCOUNTANT, and your estate planning ATTORNEY. I merely want to point out a few options for you to consider. As you know, the legal avoidance of taxes is an American tradition. How you plan to deal with matters of estate taxes is up to you and your counselors but when talking to them, consider asking about the following two strategies:

— Placing the residence in a real estate trust for the benefit of the children or grandchildren.
— Purchasing the home in the name of a grandchild who would become the landlord to whom you would pay rent. He would be taxed very little on the rental income because of his age and lack of other income. You would be able to pass the home down to your children and then to the grandchild for his use.

If considering assisted care living facilities, it will become very important for you and your children to analyze the initiation fees and up-front costs associated with the purchase (or rent). Some newer communities will allow your estate to receive the full initiation fee or apartment cost back as soon as a replacement occupant for your unit is located. For example, say you pay $ 148,000 for an apartment at XYZ Assisted Care Apartment Complex and also pay $1100 monthly as your maintenance fee. At this community, if you leave the facility or should you die, you or your estate would receive back the $ 148,000 when your apartment was rented (sold) to another occupant. At another complex, ABC Apartments, when you leave or die, YOU WOULD LOSE your initial investment (initiation fee) completely. It makes a big difference to your estate.

Regarding a mortgage on your new home, should you choose to get one. Many senior buyers are reluctant to get a mortgage for fear that they will hurt their children financially should they die before it is paid off. Well, the fact is that all or most of the mortgages that are granted today can have the principal amount covered by a mortgage insurance (term life) policy. Check with your lender to see if this protection is in place.(Formerly called mortgage insurance.)

Planning your home purchase with an eye toward the future of your estate and your children's futures is prudent and if carefully done will allow you to buy the home you want and insure that no one will say later that you "squandered" the family fortune. Yes, it is your money. And, you worked hard for it. But, let them know while you're still here that you have their best interests at heart as well.

Factor 16. Mortgages

Frequently customers come into my office and we discuss the finances necessary for them to live on a month to month basis from the income they receive from pensions and social security. Upon seeing that their income closely matches what their outlay will be, they look at each other and say "Maybe this house is too expensive for us." Obviously they are disappointed, so I ask them if they have a current mortgage on their home. Nine out of ten say NO— we paid that off three years ago. They are typically HOUSE RICH and money poor.

So often this occurs. Couples work their entire lives to get out of debt and pay off the mortgage. Then when they are no longer working and earning a big income, they must try and figure out how to AFFORD their retirement home on a fixed income.

GET A SMALL MORTGAGE.

A mortgage is the way to relieve the tight monthly pressure on your fixed income. A mortgage is the way to get those other few options that will

REALLY make you happy in this new home. The screened porch, or the whirlpool tub you always wanted. This is the time to get what you want in life. So let's figure it out.

Let's say that your entire net worth is your home which you just sold and you netted $ 137,000 after all expenses, commissions and legal fees. You have all of that amount to spend on a new home.

Your monthly pension and social security income totals $2100 combined.

The house you want costs $ 125,000 and you want to put in $30,000 in options to make it just right for you and your spouse. Can you do it?

Purchase the house with $ 110,000 down and leave $27,000 in your money market account. Apply for a mortgage of $ 50,000 which will also give you enough for closing costs as well as all of your legal expenses on the new home.

Your estimated monthly living expenses will be:

Gas	$ 75.00
Electric	55.00
Maintenance Fee	60.00
Cable	30.00
Telephone	40.00

Water and Sewer	$ 60.00
Taxes	300.00
Principal and Interest	341.00
(on $50,000 Mortgage)	
Homeowners Ins.	30.00

TOTAL MONTHLY EXPENSES   **$ 991.00**

TOTAL MONTHLY INCOME   2100

MONTHLY SPENDING RESERVE **$ 1109.00**

You can see that you should easily be able to afford to live on your income AND have the house exactly as you want it. The small mortgage is just facilitating your comfort in your retirement years. It's not a BAD thing. It's helping you to relax.

Many seniors also worry about qualifying for a mortgage at "their ages." Please be assured that there are numerous types of mortgages that you WILL be able to qualify for. Any mortgage broker or bank will be happy to give you a selection of mortgage options to choose from. Also, as we said earlier, you have the option to initiate a term life policy in place to pay off the mortgage should something unforeseen happen to you.

You've spent your life becoming debt free. Congratulations. Now you can use that financial strength to get a mortgage to become worry-free. Take advantage of this great money tool.

Factor 17. Real Estate Taxes- Reality Check

Property taxes are everywhere. At least in the United States. What you get for your tax dollar will vary from town to town but generally is dependent on the quality of your administrators and elected officials.

Schools, roads, town services, garbage collection, recreational programs, parks, police, fire, and rescue services and a multitude of other items make up the town's tax budget. The number of "ratables" in the municipality and your town's population will determine the size of your individual tax bill.

Seniors traditionally don't like to pay for services that they don't use. So, to pay for elementary schools seems a hardship since they have no school-age children. But, younger residents pay for paramedic services, and senior centers, and busing services, and these, I guess, could be looked upon in the same way if they chose too.

No matter how much you discuss it, the bottom line is "death and taxes." It's not going to change.

When you are doing your preliminary financial analysis to determine your needs relative to your choice of a senior residence and location, you must pay attention to the tax question RIGHT up front. If you are "critical" on the tax issue and if you cannot afford to pay more than a certain amount for this "cost" of your housing, then state it right away. It will directly affect the location selections that you investigate. If you must pay no more than $2000 per year in taxes, then you WILL be looking at apartment rentals or housing in the southeast or the southwest of the country. There is no way to live in Chicago or New York and pay low taxes. It's just not going to happen. So face it and move on.

When you are comparing taxes from one municipality to another, I urge you to go to the town hall and ask for the latest information on the community you are interested in. Get real numbers from the town on the model you are planning on buying. Don't rely on the assumptions of the new home salesperson. He may have outdated information.

Also look at the stability of the tax structure in the town. Find out when the last increase was and how much it was as well. Ask for projections on the next increase. Also ask about township planning and what types of rateables are on the drawing boards in the town. Attending a township meeting and planning board meeting is also a good idea if you can find the time to do so. Don't forget to confirm that garbage collection is included in the taxes. This sometimes slips through the cracks and you'll be faced with bills from a private garbage hauler. Ask about recycling and receptacles too. Are they supplied by the township or will you have to buy them?

Taxes are important. But they are only one of the factors that you will have to evaluate in your research. If you are paying more now where you currently live, consider making it a minor issue. Look at the absolute value of what you will be paying rather than a comparison between your old house and the new one. Also look at the expenses on the old house that you will no longer have to deal with such as yard maintenance and house repairs.

Factor 18. Am I too old to do this?

There will be times when you and your significant other will say things like "Are we too old to do this?" Or, "What did we get into this for?" It's only natural to stay with what's familiar and to question why you would put yourself through inconvenience, stress and pain at the later stages of your lives.

Some never move forward. Some stay in the towns they were born in— even in the same house. It's what's important to YOU. That's the difference.

Several months ago, I was in a senior community sales office and two women came in to look at our model homes. One was tall and surely was at least seventy-five years young. The other, smaller and being held up by the other's arm looked to be about eighty or eighty-five. They were both smiling when I came over to them with a chair for the smaller woman to sit in. She sat down and began to listen to me describe what they were about to see in the sales center.

During our initial conversation, I learned that they were sisters and that the younger one was actually 83 and the older one was 92. They currently lived together in a house that they had occupied for the last sixty years which was given to them when their parents died.

When I asked them the obvious question of why on earth they would put themselves through a move at their stage of life, they looked at me and then each other and the older one said, " We're tired of our old house."

Americans are blessed. And we are brave. And we are full of the most vigor and enthusiasm of any people in the world. We can do almost anything that we set our minds to at any age providing our bodies do not get in the way. Age has nothing to do with living. Realize it, and get on with the good part of your life— I call it the "next window of living."

In the next chapter, we will concentrate on the synthesis of our self-examination of needs and our field visits of communities in order to arrive at our "top two" candidates for our purchase. Activity **Steps 7 and 8** in this chapter will lead us to **Steps 9 and 10** in Chapter 10.

PRIORITIZING FACTORS

We have just reviewed 18 purchasing factors which are the most common concerns of today's senior real estate buyers. With your awareness of these factors and your ability to decide which of them will take precedence over the other, you can now begin to "focus" your selection process onto those communities or facilities that will best serve your needs.

Already in this guide you have begun to understand a lot more about what will make you and your spouse happy in your retirement years. Now we will prioritize your personal selection factors so you will be able to eliminate all communities or facilities that do not fulfill your requirements. You and your significant other have now heard about the importance of communication and you MUST continue that in this all important phase. So speak your true mind. Let your thoughts and desires be known to the other. It may make the difference between enjoying YOUR NEW HOME or just buying another house.

O.K. — Let's begin. Over the last six months

you've been to eleven communities in your home state as well as three new communities in other parts of the United States where you thought you might have interest. Your folder is bursting and you have photo upon photo of the best of the bunch. You and your spouse have spent HALF a year researching your move and now you are ready to narrow the field to the top two candidates so you can proceed with closer examination of the top contenders (Micro Research in the next chapter).

The procedure you will follow to narrow your selections must be based upon the following steps:

— Prioritize your purchase factors
— Choose your category of residence
— Rank your choices
— Make second and third visits to the top three
— Select your "Top Two"

Your primary concern elements of financial ability, health considerations, concerns for family, and fear of the unfamiliar will come first.

1. How much money do you have or can you get? And, are you willing to spend it on YOURSELF and your retirement?
2. Do your health concerns dictate a more structured medical environment for your golden years?
3. Will you let your decision to buy be impacted by your children, grandchildren, or your parents?

4. Will you choose to explore as yet untraveled roads with your spouse or by yourself or will you decide to remain among familiar albeit less than satisfying surroundings?

It's time for you to answer these questions.

Once these have been dealt with, you must prioritize the 18 factors from Chapter 8 in an order that is honest and reflects your TRUE priorities.

Following is one couple's RANKING of FACTORS showing their **MOST** important concern first:

| New Home | " I'm finally going to have a NEW home" |

| Home Design | "Price-Quality-Design-Value must be Great" |

| Community Size | "We don't want to get lost in a big place" |

| Close to Kids | " One and one half hours away AT MOST" |

| Doctors Nearby | " At our age, we want them near to us" |

| Clubhouse Size | "Doesn't matter too much to us now" |

| Town Location | "Hopefully it won't be too crowded. We'd like a friendly smaller community" |

| My Health | " Right now our health is pretty good" |

| Security Needs | "Neighbors will be security- Not gates" |

| Can we sell our house? | "It should sell fast in our town. I'm not worried about it at all" |

| Resale Values | "The market is off a little bit. But we should get enough to buy our new home" |

| Estate Planning | " We'll investigate this with our lawyer" |

| Type of Community | "Whichever feels just right to us both " |

| Taxes | "High everywhere. It's not too important" |

| HOA Concerns | "I think rules are a GOOD idea" |

| Will I work? | "I'm not sure if I'll need to work again" |

| Mortgage Needs | "We don't need to worry. We have enough to get us through without one" |

| My Age | "I feel like I'm 20. My age isn't a factor" |

This couple will be going to a well designed home in a smaller new home community that is nearby their family and new doctors yet to be picked. They have no financial concerns and feel confident formal security will not be required to make them feel safe. Since they are social, a large clubhouse is not a major issue for them either. They are a lucky couple.

Another couple might put the need for health related factors first:

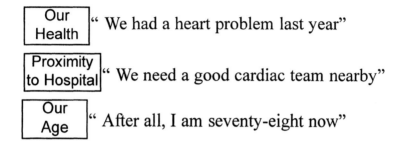

Our Health	" We had a heart problem last year"
Proximity to Hospital	" We need a good cardiac team nearby"
Our Age	" After all, I am seventy-eight now"

They might be better off looking into assisted care apartments or facilities or a mixed use complex.

Other buyers might prioritize their top factors as follows:

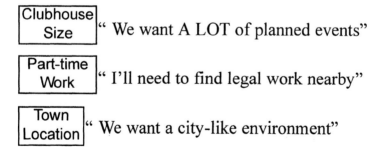

Clubhouse Size	" We want A LOT of planned events"
Part-time Work	" I'll need to find legal work nearby"
Town Location	" We want a city-like environment"

They would likely choose a large community in a more heavily populated area and might buy a new home or a resale if in good condition.

One more couple might set priorities as below:

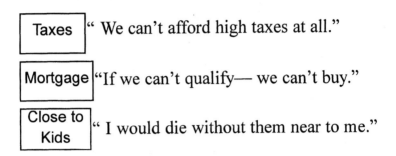

Taxes   " We can't afford high taxes at all."

Mortgage "If we can't qualify— we can't buy."

Close to " I would die without them near to me."
Kids

They will likely investigate senior apartments in towns close to their children.

The idea in setting your 18 priorities into your PERSONAL order of importance, is to establish in your own mind what is important and what is not — what is needed and what is superfluous—what meets your needs and what has no beneficial effect at all.

Once you have prioritized your purchasing criteria you will be able to select the category of retirement residence and review those communities that you have visited more closely. Or, if you haven't visited enough of the type of community you are now interested in, you can select additional sites and set about gathering more information for your folder. But, now with a more intense interest.

If, after your personal prioritization, you are positive about the selection of an active adult community for your retirement, it is time to make your second and third visits to these communities to confirm which of the eleven (or more) will be suitable for your retirement home. Second or third (return) visits can be fast or time consuming depending on how certain you are about your needs. The faster return visits are usually "fast turn-arounds" that sometimes boggle the minds of the sales people at the communities. Typically, you will enter the sales office, race past the front desk perhaps waving at the receptionist and say something like "We've been here before" — then sail into the model center. You are probably seeking simple confirmation that you DO NOT want to live in this particular community. For if you were interested, you would properly seek out your sales counselor and gather more information for your "Community Checklist Profile."

The slower second and third visits are detailed information seeking events where you find out as much as you can about the visited site. The homes, the community, the pricing, the included features, options pricing, and other pertinent information must be sought out and organized into a format that you can review at home. Work together. And USE the check lists as your information "memory jogger." If you don't find out all of this information, it could cause problems or COST you money later.

On third and even fourth visits you will usually spend a lot of time in the model(s) that you like the best. This is valuable time that you can spend "picturing" yourself living in the home. Plan a party. Get ready for weekend guests. Go to opposite ends of the home and yell to each other. LIVE IN IT for 15 to 20 minutes and you will begin to know if it is going to make you happy.

Whenever I talk about " living in the models", I think of a customer couple of mine that intrigued me every time they came into the model center. They spent six or seven visits making sure that the model they liked would be the best one for them to buy before placing their reservation deposit. After they purchased the home and while it was being constructed in the field, they would frequently come by on weekends with their friends from their old town. They would come in and go into the models and spend an hour or two each weekend showing their friends what a great place they had purchased in and what a great array of models they had to choose from.

On one rainy Saturday, I had occasion to go into the models and came upon John and Adele (my customers) who were entertaining their friends in the living room of their selected model. It was as if I stumbled into an occupied residence on any typical American street. They told me that they were "practice entertaining" prior to getting into their actual home in the community. This was wonderful, and later gave us the idea to include actual residents in our model centers. They could offer "real-life" answers to first-time visiting prospects. Visitors will tend to "believe" actual residents on a plane slightly higher than a new home salesperson who they have just met and might not yet know well enough to fully trust.

Learn to live in the models. Arrange your furniture. Watch T.V. Talk on the phone. Eat in the screened-in porch. Believe me, it works.

Third visits should result in a long "sit" with your sales counselor. He or she should be able to "budget-price" the home for you with the options that you are considering. This estimate should be capable of determining within $ 2000 what your finished home price will be. This price should include:

— Base Price of the home
— Exterior elevation premiums
— Lot premiums on your desired locations
— All standard and included features
— Major structural options
— All upgrades you are considering
— All options you are considering
— **MINUS** any incentives being offered to you.

When you are developing this budget price with the salesperson, ask if the option prices stay constant or if they can go up without notice. You may want to consider putting a clause into your purchase contract that will freeze the price of major structural options at the price quoted at the time of purchase.

A critical element in your purchase which is often left until the last minute and which often doesn't get proper attention is the selection of a lot for your home. You should spend a good deal of time with your salesperson reviewing what standard and premium lots are still available that will accommodate the model you want to build.

The selection of a lot often includes a review of the following factors which you and your spouse will have to reach agreement on before giving the builder your reservation deposit:

— What morning and afternoon sun orientation do you want. The "exposure" of the home can impact your enjoyment depending on your use of the rear porch, patio, or yard. Examine the orientation of your current home and determine what you DON'T like about the way it is positioned.

— How much are you willing to spend for a premium lot? Many feel that the money would be put to better use on options INSIDE the home such as flooring, appliances or lighting. Think about these:

— How much side yard and rear yard privacy do we need (want) ?

— Do we want to see the backs of other houses or can we afford a more private setting?

— Will a corner lot provide more privacy for us?

— Does the ground elevation make a difference to our enjoyment of the property or to our peace of mind about drainage conditions?

— Will certain locations provide quieter enjoyment of our home?

— Should we pick a lot within walking distance of the amenities on the site, the road out front, or the clubhouse with its sure to be busy parking lot?

— Will there be electrical or utility boxes on the property? And if there is, can we shrub them as we see fit to disguise the boxes?

If possible, "walk" the site with the salesperson and stand on your lot to make sure that this important decision is not made in haste.

At the third or fourth visit to the community you will want to spend some time in the facility's club-house. Ask for a pass and spend as much time in there talking to actual residents as you can. You will be meeting future neighbors and can learn a lot from these great sources of information. If they are happy in their new home and community, there is a good chance that you will be too.

Third visits and fourth visits should produce enough information for you to narrow your choices down to two communities from your eleven or more that you have seen. That is our goal. Two selected communities that will now be researched in a different way. Two communities that you will explore as a detective in order to determine which one will be YOUR NEW HOME LOCATION.

MICRO ANALYSIS OF YOUR CHOICES

You've distilled all of the information and are now down to two possible purchase locations for your retirement home. From the outside, and at a quick glance, most uneducated buyers would believe that your choice of either one would be fine. They are not as careful as you are. They are not "working" at making a sound purchase decision. They are not eliminating risks and doing their best to insure their happiness in their new home.

I'm happy that you know better.

Micro-research or analysis is derived from an economic term which simply means a detailed and focused examination of a particular phenomenon or process. Your process is the purchase of a particular home in a particular community at a particular point in time. The analysis is your careful detection and evaluation of certain facts that will confirm or deny that your selection is the best one for your needs.

The more time you have to invest in research,

the better your decision will be **EXCEPT** that construction prices will continue to rise and you will be paying more for your home. There must be a balance of research, planning, analysis, decision making, and action.

In this guide, we have suggested that an appropriate time frame for research and planning is six to eighteen months. Each case and each buyer will have different circumstances. In any case, once you have narrowed your decision to the "best few", you still have some more intense work to do.

Micro Analysis Components

After you have picked your top two locations, plan to do the following FOR EACH: (And keep notes on your findings. You will be reviewing them and comparing them to arrive at your purchase decision). I call these the top twenty-five elements. You will be able to add more to the list. Be inquisitive, be polite, and seek out as much information as you can. It will pay great dividends later.

1. Visit the community and town on different days and different hours. You will not be able to KNOW what the traffic situation is like in your new community unless you take this step. Drive rush hours and holiday weekends. Don't be surprised later by unanticipated congestion.

2. Visit the Town Hall or municipal complex.

Specifically plan to see and speak with the Tax Department and the Planning and Zoning office. You want to know exactly what the taxes will be on your new home. Ask about the tax outlook, when the next increase will be, when the last one was, and if there are any plans in the works to add or delete rateables that could affect your home's taxes. Ask the planning and zoning office about newly planned development in the town. Find out who and what is planning to come into town. If there is a major retailer already approved across the street from your community, you'd better find out now. Ask about new schools, road improvements, traffic lights, new stores, and any other changes that the township officials foresee that could affect your comfort, convenience, or tax rate. Ask for the current year's town calendar which will list all township personnel and phone numbers.

3. Buy (and possibly subscribe) to the local paper(s) that will have all of the local news and information about town issues.

4. Visit the town's main library. Ask the people who work there about the town. What is good? What is not so good? Library personnel are usually very polite and accommodating to visitors.

5. Drive the area. Find the stores, the hospitals, the doctors and butchers and dry cleaners. Speak with the local shopkeepers and the town barber (while getting a haircut) about the town and the adult community you are considering. Don't be shy about your interest in getting as up to date as you can about hot topics in town.

6. Visit the Police Department. Ask if they have a printed report about major crimes reported in the township over the last three years. Normally they are required to keep these records. Also they should be able to give you a percentage of "crimes solved" in the town.

7. Eat in as many different restaurants in the town as you can. Find out for yourselves where the "really best" places to eat can be found.

8. Stay at the local hotel or motel overnight. Visit your community at night and monitor noise and activity levels there. Is the clubhouse open? Is it active?

9. Spend intensive hours with the sales counselor that you have now come to know and trust. Ask everything you can about the homes, the builder, the quality, the site improvements, the homeowner's association, the planting guidelines, the complaints of residents, water drainage, and any other topics that you can think of that might be of consequence to you at some point in time.

10. Meet the builder if you have not already done so. You have a right to meet the owner/developer. Ask your sales counselor. He will get it arranged.

11. Talk to actual residents on the street, in the clubhouse, at their front doors, or anywhere else you see them. They are your most honest and believable source of information about difficulties in the community. Ask about water drainage, garbage pick-up, the developer's maintenance crew, the builder's warranties, the operation of the homeowner's association.

Be as inquisitive as you can be and get informed with information you can trust.

12. Go to church at the nearest location and talk to the priest or pastor or rabbi about the town and the community.

13. Call the Chamber of Commerce. Find out about the benefits of living and working in the town.

14. Call the Better Business Bureau of the corporate headquarter's location and ask for a complaint report on the builder of your community.

15. Ask the sales representative for the name of a bank reference for the builder. They may even volunteer this information with a sign on the community site indicating which bank "financed" the project. Ask for the name of a Vice-President. You want to get a reference on the builder before you buy. If the company is public, remember all you may get is an annual report. But—try.

16. Ask for an "Option Selection Preview" to more closely outline what options you would purchase for your new home. If the selection coordinator has the time she or he may be able to schedule a "short" presentation to get you more acclimated to the products being offered to you.

17. Measure the house "exactly". Make sure your furniture will fit. Ask the sales counselor if the builder will accommodate minor changes to the home if needed to accommodate special pieces.

18. Estimate the cost of window and wall treatments that you will probably purchase later. You may

even get permission to have a window, closet, painting, or other outside contractor in to "price up" your requirement from the model in the sales center.

19. Ask to see a home under construction at various stages of development. Some builders offer construction tour events to "show-off" their quality levels.

20. Ask for the exact names of the construction materials vendors so you can call them and ask for a "spec sheet" on the materials being used on your home. If you are not familiar with fiberglass shingles, or vinyl windows, or insulated slab construction, it is a good idea to become familiar with these products or processes BEFORE you buy.

21. Research your financial assistance requirements. Ask the sales counselor for mortgage brokers that they recommend.

22. Pin down what the exact "closing costs" will be for your home.

23. Ask to fully read the Public Offering Statement. Usually the salesperson can make this available for you to read in his office prior to purchasing the home.

24. Take the salesperson into the model and MAKE him or her point out all of the options in the house. Don't ASSUME lighting, special floor treatments, shelving, cabinets, or any other fixture is included in the price. Find out for sure.

25. Ask for a copy of ALL resident newsletters that may have been printed prior to your purchase. Usually the current month's issue is available. But earlier issues may point out problems in the communi-

ty that have been resolved or that may still be of a concern.

Micro Research will make you more of an expert on the town and community than the residents or the builder's sales personnel and it will greatly reduce your stress level during the purchase procedures that will follow.

An important consideration of seniors is transportation services that are available "just in case" you decide that you do not want to drive anymore. You should look into the township services, the county services, the homeowners association "sunshine committee" services, local cab and bus services, public transportation terminal locations and any other public or private mechanism for use by you if you decide it's time to sell the car.

Visit the post office and find out all of the details about how you will transfer mail if you move there. Some post offices will allow you to use the new address BEFORE you move in. You simply pick up mail when you are visiting the home being constructed. When you close on the new house, simply tell the postal clerk to start sending it to the house. It works.

County governments usually have senior services that you should be aware of as well. Contact the senior organizations in your new county and find out about these services. Also find out from each organization what your membership in their organization involves. You may find that you are already able to join formed groups that pertain to your existing or new interests. Take the time to explore all of the possibilities of retirement. Read the papers and call the authors or advertisers if you see something that might be appealing to you.

Your micro research as outlined in this chapter will be time consuming. That's why we want to restrict it to your top two community choices. But, if you allocate your time properly, and use a weekly calendar to map out your trips and activities, you should be able to survive the ordeal. Also, consider splitting up the research with your spouse. Head off in different directions and then compare notes at dinner. It will cut the research time in half and you will find that it can be a lot of fun too.

In the next chapter we will discuss your actual decision to buy the home of your choice. This is **Step 11** of your purchase procedure. This is the easiest chapter and the hardest activity. YOU control the planned timing of your purchase. But, often powers out of our control make the decision commitment a gut wrenching task. I have brought you to this point. Now you must decide if you are going to make your move.

In Chapter Twelve will will fully detail the buying procedures you will be encountering (**STEP 12**).)

MAKING THE DECISION TO BUY
(Step 11)

Eight or eighteen months of planning and research and now you are pretty sure that you know where you want to live out your next thirty years.

Using the planning and activity steps from previous chapters, you have decided that you are going to buy a **specific** model in a **specific** community in a **specific** town by a **specific** date and that you will be spending a **specific** amount of money in a **specific** way. You are READY to put down a deposit.

You and your spouse leave the house in the morning and one of you says, " Do you have the checkbook, honey?" The other says nothing but goes back to the kitchen desk and grabs it. As you drive, you talk a little about something the grandkids said the day before, or talk about the messy neighbor that never sweeps up the grass after he mows, or talk about where you want to have dinner that night. You talk about anything at all because you are really getting nervous about what is about to happen when you step into that salesperson's office and say that you want to buy a home TODAY.

It is natural to be nervous. Especially with a decision that you have spent so much time making. But, you persevere and park the car and go into the sales center for the fifth time and ask for your sales counselor who you have now come to know and like.

" What can I do for you today, folks?"

Usually, your response will be anything but, Here's a check for $2500, lets get this home rolling." Rather, you'll probably say that you want to cover a few more questions or options or items relating to the purchase that are still unclear. You may want to review pricing one more time and make sure that you're getting any special incentives that the builder might be offering at that particular point in time. Then you'll say that you want to take another quick look at the models and that you'll be back.

A quality salesperson will know why you are there and why you are nervous. He or she will not rush you or hassle you or run after you with a pen and a reservation form. A good salesperson will wait for you to be ready BEFORE he asks for the check.

When customers return from the model as in the case above, I usually conduct myself as follows to SEE if they are ready to get out their checkbooks:

I call them into my office if I am free or I signal them as they wait on the outside couch when I am done with the people in my office. They enter and sit comfortably on the two chairs opposite me. As they get seated, I clear off my entire desk and put a blank yellow pad of paper and a pen in front of me and look at them both and say, " What questions do you still have that I can help you with?" This is usually followed by a few questions about the house, or some minor item that is really not a major consideration to them at this time. They are just trying to eliminate the inertia that is so common at this point. After a few seconds of silence, one will say, " Explain how this purchase procedure works. What money do we need to put down to get this rolling?" And, indeed the process of purchasing has begun.

I will then completely explain reservation deposits, agreements of sale, attorney review, sale of home contingencies, mortgage contingencies and the benefits and risks of purchasing on a non-contingent basis. Further, I will explain what monies will be due when and what the customer can expect in terms of timing of activities and completion date of the home. I will cover the process quickly and professionally so that the buyer doesn't become overwhelmed but merely well informed. After that I will ask them if they are ready to proceed. And, if I've been convincing and competent they usually say yes.

The work ahead is not easy to understand and

can be confusing for many who have not had a lot of business or financial experience in their lives. It is up to the salesperson to make everything clear. It must be done accurately and it must be done well or the deal will fall apart.

Most builders or developers will have a reservation policy whereby the buyer can put down a refundable deposit to hold a lot and the home price for a three day to seven day period. This gives them a chance to think through their final decision and change their minds without risk of losing their deposit. There is always a percentage of reservations that are cancelled for one reason or another. Better salespeople have better ratios of cancelled reservations than do poor salespeople. For if he has explained things well and prepared his well informed customer properly, there is little chance of cancellation except for significant personal changes that may have occurred in the buyer's lives.

The decision to place a reservation deposit IS THE DECISION TO BUY and once that is done the process that follows is merely mechanics.

Following is a list of reasons why buyers might cancel a reservation or in other words change their minds about buying. As you read them, I think you will smile because you are already well past these feelings that can only come about by not being properly prepared or by not doing the necessary self evaluation and research that you have adopted into YOUR search methodology. You will not cancel your reservations because you have read and lived this planning guide:

Typical Reasons Reservations are Cancelled:

Reason # 1. Buyers get panicked by the thought of change and retreat to the comfort of their existing home.

Reason # 2. Their children or parents "go crazy" when they tell them about the purchase they have just made. They make them feel guilty about the move.

Reason # 3. They decide that adult living is too restrictive. (Usually there's a reason behind this).

Reason # 4. Attorney tells them they should sell their house BEFORE they buy the new home.

Reason # 5. They suddenly hear about a "better place." (This is a procrastination opportunity).

Reason # 6. They can't wait for construction of a new home. They decide to buy a resale.

Reason # 7. They find out that there is a landfill behind the community.

Reason # 8. The taxes are too high.

Reason # 9. They speak to a resident who tells them that there is water problems in the community.

Reason # 10. They find that the rules and regulations are too strict. They don't want to live in that kind of control.

Reason # 11. They find that their finances won't allow them to buy at this particular time.

Reason # 12. They have sudden health problems and may have to have major surgery.

Reason # 13. The husband or wife just doesn't

have the same degree of commitment to the move as does the other. (They should have found this out months before).

Reason # 14. A child is moving back into the parent's home due to divorce.

Reason # 15. The parents have to lend a considerable sum of money to a child for a business or personal problem.

Reason # 16. They have just decided to put a parent into a nursing home and have money concerns.

Reason # 17. A brand new community has just been announced and it "sounds like" it will just be perfect. (Another slant on Reason # 5).

Reason # 18. The daughter of the buyer has announced her wedding plans and they include the use of the house they were going to sell.

I'll stop here because I know you have an idea of what all of the typical reasons are for cancelling. Some are very valid and can cause a painful delay in your move because of factors that are out of your control. Others though, arise from a "premature" decision to purchase, or from poor communication between spouses, or just plain lack of research.

Unlike yourselves, some buyers don't do their homework. They don't evaluate their needs, assess their conditions, discuss their true likes and dislikes, or in any way prepare for the home purchasing process.

I said that this chapter would be easy and I meant it. But, it was only easy because you've taken the time to be well prepared for it. — Nice work.

PART II

AFTER THE

PURCHASE

Chapter Twelve

PURCHASE AGREEMENTS AND CONTINGENCIES
(Step 12)

You've just left the sales office and you're a little bit shaky. The salesperson said that you had seven days to change your mind, but it doesn't seem to help. You're nervous. At the same time, however, you are relieved. For after so many months of research and planning, you are pretty sure that your decision was a good one. While you are at lunch, you review what will happen next. Will you need a lawyer? How do you start getting rid of all the stuff in your home? What real estate broker should you use to sell the house? In fact, SHOULD you sell your house first or wait until the new one is finished.

In the chapters that follow in Part Two of this planning guide, we will try and assist you with some of your concerns about what should happen AFTER the purchase. For as sound as your decision to buy may be, it can be spoiled if you do not know what is to follow the RESERVATION DEPOSIT.

Let's begin with the mechanics of your legal agreement with the builder. It begins with the reservation deposit and ends with the closing of title to your new home. While the legal items may vary from builder to builder, the following is a more or less probable list of "paper" that you should get ready to see in the next several weeks. **(Remember to consult your real estate attorney for any specific recommendations or procedures that will insure your maximum protection for this considerable purchase.)**

The Reservation Deposit

The reservation deposit at most adult communities will have a no-risk three to seven day cancellation period where you are allowed to change your mind and not purchase. Because of the magnitude of this decision, most builders understand that you may require a little time to digest what you have just done. This also saves them the cost of entering into costly legal review discussions with a buyer that may be inclined to cancel in a few days or weeks. While YOU have prepared well for the decision and will be sure of your choice when you reserve, a percentage of your friends will not and may be stricken with "second thoughts" or other types of buyer's anxiety and decide to cancel.

The typical reservation deposit will require a check for $1000 to $3000 which may or may not be deposited into the builder's escrow account as a refundable earnest money downpayment. Make sure there are no strings attached to this deposit money and make sure that the deposit is recorded on a reservation form which you are copied with before leaving the sales office. It's also a good idea to get a copy of your check as well.

The Agreement of Sale

Approximately one week after your reservation deposit it will be time to enter into a formal agreement of sale with the builder. At this juncture you will sign (execute) one to several copies of a legal purchase agreement. You will usually leave with one copy for yourselves, and a second one for your attorney to review. The builder will retain one to several signed copies for his records. The agreement will consist of a number of standard pages and may have one or several "addendums" which are required because of the type of agreement you are signing or because of legal requirements of the town or the state's Real Estate Commission or other governing agencies concerned with the sale of real estate.

Attorney Review

Attorney review periods vary in the different states and may also vary depending on the type of community or facility where you are purchasing. Consult your attorney for the exact time allowance for attorney review in your state.

Attorney review is that period of time when

your real estate attorney may read, review, comment, and negotiate changes to your agreement in an effort to protect your interests or in an effort to modify the contract to bring you greater advantage in the purchase. Typically attorney review periods can last from one day to several weeks if there are a lot of questions to be resolved.

Usually when you drop off or mail your contract to your attorney he will immediately send a letter to the builder's attorney and "open the lines" of communication between the two parties. This is all that is required of you as long as your attorney is diligent and responds to the builder's attorney requests and correspondence. But, YOU must insure that the communication is free flowing. There have been times when attorneys have "dropped the ball" and buyers found themselves OUT of attorney review without their concerns being addressed. This is rare as most attorneys are diligent and responsible, but I want you to stay on top of the process for your own protection.

Types of Agreements

The Agreement of Sale may reflect either a noncontingent or a contingent purchase of your new home. The difference between these two types must be completely understood by you before you reserve your lot.

Non-Contingent Purchase Agreement

Perhaps the simplest of agreements, the non-contingent type is structured so that you buy the home with a ten or twenty percent downpayment, select your options when instructed, and close title on your new home at a future date that you have specified with the builder.

In order to qualify for this type of of purchase, you must have the financial capability "in hand" to buy the home and options OUTRIGHT without the need to sell your existing house or qualify for a mortgage. It is indeed a luxurious way to purchase and is most often reserved for buyers that are first timers, those that are buying a second home, and those that are financially well off enough to make this significant financial expenditure.

For the buyer WITH an existing home to sell, the benefit of buying on a non-contingent basis is that they will be able to hold off selling the old house until the new home is ready for their occupancy, thus eliminating the need for temporary housing and furniture storage. They can decide when to market their old house but must remember that if they do not sell it before the new one closes, THEY WILL HAVE TWO HOUSES to maintain and pay taxes on. Because of the significant financial exposure fewer than thirty percent of active adult buyers are capable of this type of purchase. Some buyers who are capable of carrying the old house as well as a mortgage on the new one will buy on a non-contingent basis and then "time" the listing of their house and subsequent closing to try and match the closing date on the new home. This is a neat trick if you can do it.

The Contingent Contract of Sale

Far more likely is a **contingency** on a purchase agreement. Here, there is a condition placed upon the Agreement of Sale for the buyer's protection.

Following are the three most common contingencies for your review:

Sale of Home Contingency
The builder will allow the buyer a certain period of time to SELL his old house before the new one will be started. If the old house does not sell, the contract is made null and void, usually without monetary penalty to the buyer.

An earnest money deposit of up to ten percent may or may not be required when this type of contingency is executed.

Mortgage Contingency
The builder will allow the buyer a certain period of time to obtain a mortgage commitment from a suitable lender that will make the buyer CAPABLE of proceeding with the full purchase of the new home.

Often, the builder will reserve the right to obtain a mortgage FOR THE BUYER if he is unable to obtain one himself. If the mortgage or mortgage approval is not obtained the contract becomes null and void (usually at no penalty to the buyer.)

An earnest money deposit of up to ten percent may or may not be required when this type of contingency is executed.

Closing Contingency

If the buyers first house is sold and there is a firm closing date on settlement, the builder may allow a special sale of home contingency which is called a closing contingency. Here, the builder will allow up to the scheduled date of the closing on the first house for the buyer to commence the start of the new home at the new community. If the closing is delayed for too long a period, or if the deal falls through altogether, the builder will make the contract null and void and the buyer again will be released usually without penalty.

An earnest money deposit of up to ten percent may or may not be required when this type of contingency is executed.

Other types of contingencies may be offered by the builder and a separate addendum to the agreement of sale would be executed at contract signing time.

Bumping Contingent Contracts

Some builders in certain communities will be pleased to offer you a contingent contract subject to the sale of your existing home. They will be pleased to hold the lot and price on the new home for you until you have sold your house and are ready to proceed with construction. BUT the contract body or the sale of home contingency addendum may contain a clause that allows the builder to "bump" you off of your lot if a CASH buyer presents a non-contingent offer and is ready to proceed with immediate construction. This is good business for the builder because he can "fill in" his community lots rather than leave gaps in the rows of homes. It is BAD for you because now you have to re-select from a declining inventory of homesites. Be sure to ask your sales counselor if "bumping" is going to occur at your community.

Form of the Agreement of Sale

Whatever the type of Agreement of Sale, in most states, the form of it will usually consist of the following items:
— Real Estate Agency Disclosure Statement
— Agreement of Sale **Cover Sheet** summarizing the price and terms of the agreement.
— Paragraph on the Buyers Right To Cancel.

(This is also known as the **Recision Period**— the right to cancel for any reason for a specified period of time).

— Body of the Standard Agreement
— Contingency Addendums(SOHC/Mortgage)
— Standard Contract Addendums
— Real Estate Agency Addendums
— Special Addendums if required
— Signature and Witness pages
— Standard Features Listings
— Construction Specifications
— Estimate of Closing Costs
— Title Insurance and Survey Addendums
— Options Addendums (if selections completed)

The salesperson with whom you sign the Agreement of Sale should generally review the content of the contract during your signing appointment. As you can see from the above, there is a lot to review and you should seek counsel during the recision period for the complete review of the contract.

(Author note:)

(Customers always ask me if they should get an attorney. I always say the same thing. I tell them that they are spending $ 150,000 on the last major purchase of their lives. They quickly see the importance and ask their accountant or banker or stock broker for a real estate attorney referral.)

Additions to the Agreement of Sale

After your attorney review period ends and perhaps even after the new home construction begins, there will be other legal papers to be signed by you and the builder. Below are the most common ones:

— Release of Sale of Home Contingency (Addendum).

This will be signed when you are ready to pay additional required deposit monies and have your home construction begin. You must "release" the builder from this contingency before he will start your home.
— Release of the Mortgage Contingency (Addendum).

When official word is heard that your mortgage or mortgage approval has been granted, you will release the builder from this contingency and pay the additionally required deposits to begin construction of your home.

— Release of Closing Contingency (Addendum).

After you close on the old house, you are ready to proceed with the new one. Release this contingency, pay your required additional deposits and pick your colors and options. Your new home will begin.

— Options Addendum

Usually, your new home construction will only begin after you have picked out all of your exterior and interior colors and ordered the options that you want included. Typically, your **options addendum** will become part and parcel of your Agreement of Sale. Most builders will require from half to all of options money "fronted" when you order them. For this reason, it is important enough to be addressed in the initial attorney review process, rather than at a later date. I recommend that if you are considering "expensive structural options" in your home that you try and have the builder "freeze" the price of same at the original signing of the Agreement of Sale so that future options increases can be avoided. This will be handled with a "special addendum" to the Agreement of Sale.

— Lot or Model Switch Addendums

Before the home has been started, some builders may allow you to change the house model or the lot of your choice or some other feature of your purchase. This will usually be handled by a standard addendum specially suited to the request. A LOT SWITCH for example is a common one. It is always subject to availability. If executed, this will become part of the Agreement of Sale and supercedes the original selection of a lot. Once a building permit has been ordered, most builders will not allow this kind of a change. So make sure of your lot and model style as soon as you can— preferably at time of reservation deposit.

Other Important Agreement Components

The Estimate of Closing Costs

At the time of your Agreement of Sale, you should be entitled to know what your approximate closing costs are going to be on the new home. Ranging from $ 0.00 to over $ 3000, these numbers will be important to you. Ask your salesperson about them if they are not part of your contract.

The Recision Period (Your RIGHT to cancel)

Whether it be three days or seven days, make sure that you understand the requirements of notification if you decide to cancel your contract. Also be aware if certain documents that you have been presented with need to be returned before you will receive your refunded deposit monies. Also, ask the salesperson about the length of time required for the return of deposits should you decide not to proceed.

The Public Offering Statement

In most states, if the size of the residential project is large and if customers are being solicited from a national pool of buyers, there will be a state requirement or real estate agency requirement to provide a Public Offering Statement (Public Disclosure Statement) which must be made available for review at the offices of the builder and must be presented to buyers at the time they execute their Agreement of Sale. This document has information about the project, the builder, the community, the owners association, operating budgets if there is one in place, rules and regulations of the community and a variety of other information that is essential to the full understanding of the community where the buyer is about to become a resident. It is important that you receive this document, if required by law. Ask your salesperson if the document does exist at your community. And READ it.

Warranties on Home Quality

The stated and expressed warranties of the builder must be in a format that can become part of the Agreement of Sale. Whether or not the warranties are in the brochure or on a separate piece of paper doesn't really matter. But they must be printed somewhere.

Homeowner 10-15 Year Warranties

Most builders today offer some kind of extended five, ten, or longer homeowner's warranty. You should be receiving documents at the signing of the Agreement of Sale which outlines these in complete detail. You should also ask for a sample policy for review so you will know EXACTLY what is covered by the policy and what is not. You also want to insure that the cost is fully born by the builder and not shared by you.

Survey Stakes

You will have to decide if you want survey stakes or not. In most adult communities, stakes are not required because normally you are not allowed to construct fences or sheds on your property. But, if you are planning an addition or patio expansion on your home AFTER you move in, you might want to have the corners of your lot marked in some manner.

Well, that about concludes what you will encounter in the reservation to final contract phase of your purchase. The attorney review period should bring up most of the important considerations that your lawyer has about the contract and the addendums that you have signed as they relate to your legal protection.

The key points that follow are important for you to discuss with your attorney and UNDERSTAND before you are out of attorney review and in a binding contract. They are a sampling of items that frequently come up in the review process at adult communities. Discussing them before you buy may save you aggravation and money later on:

1. What guarantees do I have that my home will be completed on time? Can I penalize the builder if he is late?

2. What penalties will accrue to me if I delay the

closing of title? Are there "time is of the essence" clauses?

3. Can I lock in the price of structural options at the time of initial contract? Regular options?

4. Do I have to have an attorney at the closing of title? Can a title company do the settlement?

5. What inspections will I be allowed to conduct on my home while it is under construction?

6. What is my guarantee that the builder will not default on the project?

7. Will my deposit monies accrue interest for me during construction?

8. Will I be able to change my mind on ordered options before they are installed?

9. Can I use my own flooring contractors to save money? Will they be permitted on the job?

10. Can I install an intercom system in my home while it is under construction?

11. Can I sell my home myself and still get the sale of home contingency benefits?

12. What happens if one of us dies while the home is being constructed? What will my recourse be?

I want you to ask questions when you are in attorney review. Be fair but be informed. You owe it to yourself. And, remember, your salesperson can answer a lot of these before you go to contract.

After the contract has made it through attorney review, the lawyers will exchange correspondence that says the contract is firm and both parties are committed to the other. Then you will take the next step depending on which type of contract you have negotiated. If you are non-contingent, you will schedule your selections and the house construction will begin. If you are contingent, you will embark on the sale of your existing house or get your mortgage approval in process or await your closing on the old house if that's the contingent item. In any case, you will not start your house until you "release" the contingency item. After release, the options selection process occurs and the building permit is ordered for your new home.

From that point forward, you will more or less become a spectator and will "watch" your home being built. There will not be a lot of legal requirements or papers to sign during this phase. You are now just awaiting the completion of the home and the Closing of Title.

The Closing (Settlement on your new home)

The closing of title also called the settlement is the day when ownership of your new home transfers from the builder to you. In return, you are presenting the builder with all the monies due for the home and any options ordered. You will pay any association fees that are due and of course the real estate taxes that may be due to the township tax collector.

The closing usually takes place at an attorney's

office or at the on-site closing room at the community where you are purchasing. It can take from ten minutes to a few hours depending on whether or not you are getting a mortgage from a lender other than the builder. Frequently, if not always, it is preceded by a complete and comprehensive inspection of your home to make sure that it is EXACTLY as you have ordered it. Options, quality of construction, color schemes, operation of all elements and any other items that you deem important are checked by you PRIOR to sitting at the closing table.

Some ten days to two weeks before you "close" on your home, you will receive a settlement sheet from the builder or from your attorney and you will be instructed what monies to bring and what kind of checks to use and any other information that will be required for the closing to run smoothly. An attorney usually has you make a check payable to his escrow account and then he makes disbursements at the closing table out of his checkbook.

When the "money part" of the closing is over, the builder representative usually reviews important information about your new home and will give you a "package" of warranties, keys, garage door openers, phone numbers, and any other items that are important to you as a new homeowner. And, that's about it. It really is simple as long as everyone has done their job, and the paperwork has been delivered on time. If you're lucky, after the closing, you may be presented with a gift from your salesperson for being such patient and friendly buyers.

In this chapter I have tried to present a simple overview of what you can look forward to in the contract phase of your purchase. Your salesperson is your guide. You should learn to rely upon him or her for input, answers, and exact data that will give you the information you need to make sensible decisions. But, remember, that the salesperson works for the builder and also that they are usually very busy trying to get reservation deposits. The responsibility is yours to MAKE SURE that everything is on track to a successful conclusion.

As I stated to you earlier in this guide, you have to establish a close working and open dialogue with your real estate attorney, your accountant, your stock broker, and your estate planner to make sure that this home purchase is done correctly.

In the next chapter, we will begin to examine the interactions with another professional group of people that can make or BREAK your purchase. The real estate broker that you pick to sell your existing home is VERY important. Choose him or her wisely.

SELLING THE OLD HOUSE—THE CHOICES

For active adults planning to move into a new retirement setting, perhaps one of the most difficult aspects of the task is mustering the courage to clean out and sell the old house. After all, there may be thirty or more years of living to be collected out of basements, attics, closets, and even kitchen cabinets. It is an awesome task. Very often, the thought of "throwing out" memories of the children's growing years or favorite articles collected over many decades of married life is enough for a couple to call off their purchase entirely. It is a psychological challenge to say the least.

Most will live through the experience however and will make it to their new, clean, smaller home with less pain than they anticipated. Most will realize that the move is right and that "things" have to take a back seat to their comfort and happiness.

Once the decision has been made to buy and the reservation deposit has been placed, those buyers with a sale of home contingency in their agreement of sale must now begin the process of selecting a real estate broker who will hopefully sell their house. But, how will they know how to begin? How will they know which broker will work best for them? How will they know what list price will be right and yield the "after commission" amount they need to buy their new home? And how will they insure that it is sold BEFORE the sale of home contingency expires? For, wouldn't if be awful if they couldn't move to their dream home because they were unable to sell the old house?

Before we outline what Proper Real Estate Brokerage SHOULD entail in Chapter Fourteen, we must first cover a few topics that will serve to "update you" on the current state of the industry. After reading the following five short sections, we will look in more depth as what you should expect from a reputable real estate broker.

The Market (and World) Has Changed

Prior to the 1970's things were a little simpler. Handshake agreements, the value of "a person's word", good faith and credit policies at banks and businesses were common, and the principal of *caveat emptor* or buyer beware ruled most real estate transactions.

Prior to the seventies, there was also less regard for the environmental dangers of our world and we were not too concerned about drinking water quality, chemical impact on the environment or the maximum protection of bird and wildlife populations.

During this earlier time, there was also about two thirds less lawyers that we have today and the litigious propensities that exist now where one can be sued at the drop of a hat for anything at all did not exist yet.

When selling a house today, you will face a whole new set of circumstance than you did in 1970. The primary reason for the change is the worldwide sociologic switch from the policy of buyer beware to that of consumer protection. Since Ralph Nader began his quest to make the automobile safer for Americans, we have all had to become more cognizant of how we advertise our products and services so that the BUYER is protected from false claims and worse, a product that fails entirely.

I remember selling a house of mine in 1979. I had built the home myself in 1976. It was a beautiful brick colonial on a lovely river in a New Jersey shore town. When it was built, I had air conditioning registers put into each room but I did not install a central air conditioning system in the attic. I was making it "ready" for the air conditioning unit for a later installation of the unit should I decide it was necessary.

Well, the breezes off of the river were great, and

the brick exterior and excellent insulation sheltered us enough so that we never had to add the A/C unit at all.

When it came time to list the house for sale, I called in a local broker who did her inspection and filled out the listing sheet as she normally would have. When she saw that each room had an air conditioning register and knowing that we had hot water baseboard heat, she inaccurately recorded on the listing form that the house had central air conditioning.

Within weeks, the house sold for full price. We went to settlement and everything was fine until I got a call from the broker. She told me that the new owner felt as if he was deceived when he learned that the air conditioning unit was not installed in the house.

I explained that it wasn't my intention to deceive anyone. I hadn't ever thought about the air conditioning unit. We had never discussed it either. In fact, I never even reviewed the listing description with the broker. I pleaded ignorance and offered no accommodation to the buyer. After all, it was HIS responsibility to know what he was buying. It was BUYER BEWARE. And that was fine back then. I never heard another word about the matter. No lawyers were called. It died. I was so lucky.

Today's seller has to make sure that every aspect of the house is reported accurately. Full disclosure of problems must be made. The days of putting a coat of paint over a leaky basement floor to hide water marks are gone. Today, the buyer is the king and he usually gets every protection the law will afford.

In many states, the normal protections for the buyer may include:

— A full condition disclosure form that the seller has to fill out at the time the home is listed. Any known problems with the house must be identified. This is a signed record of the seller's knowledge of the house. If he misleads the buyer in any way the penalties later on can be severe and costly.

— A disclosure on the presence of lead based paints or other harmful substances.

— An independent home inspection which will fully examine and report on EVERY aspect of the building structure and contents. This inspection can be very punishing on an older home as most inspectors are "trying" to point out any faults that might exist. Most inspectors are reputable and knowledgeable and will recognize that older homes may not " take" severe testing of plumbing systems for example. The buyer should "guide" the inspector to a gentler review if the home is over forty years old.

— Requested replacement of house components that are deemed unsafe or out of date based upon the aforementioned inspection. (subject to seller approval)

— Seller warranties (30,60,or 90 days)

— Homeowners warranties (up to a year)

— Required inspection by environmental

agencies (local, or state) if there is evidence of contamination or spillage into underground water sources or neighboring streams or adjacent bodies of water.

— Wetlands reviews and certifications if there is evidence that the property is or was even partially associated with a wetlands condition.

— A myriad of legal requirements that may be placed upon the home seller by the buyer's attorney, the realtor's attorney, or even municipal agencies if the zoning or conditional uses of the property are to be changed or grandfathered by the new owner.

As is clear, you have a lot more to concern yourself with today when you sell your home. As we approach the year 2000 it will only get more complex. So plan to use a quality broker, get a quality attorney, and hope that the home inspection doesn't leave you in shock or pounding your fist through the sheetrock.

Resale Market Realities

Real estate agents like to make money. That should come as no surprise to you. In fact, the desire to make a lot of money is at the core of most of our activities throughout our lives. It's not a bad thing.

But, with the sale of your house, we want you to do a careful analysis of your selection process when selecting a real estate agent to represent you. Someone aggressive but someone fair as well.

As with all professional groups, you will find that there are good members and bad members. The secret is for you to know enough about what makes a good one so that you can tell these two groups apart.

While I have spent most of my selling life in new home communities, I have met many resale real estate agents over the years and, like many of you, have likely formed a stereotyped image of them. I know that there are great ones that are at the top of their class and who you would even recommend to your own family members. But, there also seems to be a lot of part-time people selling real estate too. Part-time means that they are doing something else that may be equally important all the other times. That may make it seem as though they are always preoccupied with something else — thinking about matters other than selling your house. Are these types of sales people the exception? I hope so for your sake.

In the next chapter, we'll discuss GOOD real estate practices conducted by GOOD agents. But right now, I want to warn you about the not so great real estate agents. I do this for educational reasons. I want you to be wary of agents that are not interested in your best interest. This may help you to appreciate the ones that do have your house sale and your needs as their first priority. The following signals are not exact indicators of poor performance, but I urge you to be careful if your agent or his broker exhibit any of these characteristics either before or after the listing of your home:

— They are not punctual for appointments.

— They preview your home in less than fifteen minutes and quote you a probable selling price.

— They produce a Comparative Market Analysis of your home at the first visit.

— They seem disorganized and unattentive.

— They do not listen to what you are telling them about your home or your needs.

— They do not first find out why you are selling and what your plans are for your next residence.

— They promise a discounted commission if you will list with them.

— They do not answer your phone calls.

— They do not give you a written proposal and a written advertising plan for your property.

— They ask you for more than a six month listing agreement.

— They will not allow a three month cancellation if they do not perform as they have promised.

— They do not do an open house for other brokers and the public.

— They do not produce a brochure on your home to leave with visitors and other brokers.

— They are not members of the local Board of Realtors.

— They do not list your home at no charge on the Internet.

— They are not willing to cooperate with other brokers and split their commission fairly.

— They do not put your home in M.L.S.

The real estate agents that I want you to be wary of are the ones that are so anxious to "list" your house, that they may rush to judgement and not carefully evaluate the listing price level. If you list too high, your traffic will suffer. If you list too low, your net proceeds will not be adequate for your next move. There must be a balance of price and your motivation to sell with your financial condition in mind.

If I were a good (or a bad) sales agent in the resale market and you called me up to tell me that you were thinking about selling your home, I would certainly ask you the following questions immediately:

1. How long have you lived there?
2. Did you buy the home new?
3. What are your reasons for selling?
4. Is the home in good condition?
5. When do you feel you want to sell?
6. Have you spoken to any other brokers yet?

If I were a BAD sales agent and if your answer to number 1. above was that you had been in the home for over thirty years (as many of you have), I would most certainly try and set up an appointment for the next afternoon or sooner. I would wear my best blue suit, listen to you talk about your house and all the things that you have done to it over the past twenty years, and might be listening for signals from you as to what you THOUGHT the house was worth.

Then, perhaps after coffee and cake, I would give you a suggested listing price which (coincidently) matched your expectations. After getting my six month exclusive listing, you would wave goodbye to me at the front door and say to each other, "What a nice man. And isn't it great that our house IS worth what we thought."

I would have done my job. I would have gotten the listing. And without even having to promise how much advertising I would do. Without even having to do a comparative market analysis of similar homes. Without any effort at all, I was now assured of making my commission on the sale. Now, no matter who managed to sell the house, my broker and I would get our split out of the deal. No matter how many reductions in price I would have to talk you into, my income was secured. Without any regard for your goals or needs, I looked successful. But, what success did I bring to you.

Good agents have to be sensitive to your needs. The days of fast and loose real estate are over. You need professionals who are going to be counselors to you as well as salespeople.

I recall a true instance that will explain this a little more.

Barry and his Mom wanted to move into a community at which I worked, and they signed a reservation deposit and then a contract to purchase. They lived in a home that was fifty-one years old in a good section of a good town with excellent schools, shopping, hospitals and police and fire services. It was a nice, safe town with great neighbors. They had paid $ 1500 for the home new. That's fifteen hundred dollars, fifty-one years ago.

They called in a local real estate agent to look at the house. After about twenty minutes, he suggested that the house list for about $ 150,000 but only after they replaced the roof, the furnace, some of the wood flooring and all of the appliances in the kitchen. He would get the listing started, but they should start calling contractors right away. He was seeking an EASY sale and a fast commission.

Before Barry listed the house, he asked me what he should fix in his house BEFORE listing it with a real estate broker. I suggested that because it was a fifty-one year old house, the likely buyer would be renovating it extensively anyway and that they should get some better opinions first before they spent what limited capital they had to get the house ready for sale.

We were working with a home marketing assistance company at that time and they were engaged to select two brokers from Barry's town to go into the house and do comprehensive comparative market analysis of the home. I will outline how this procedure works in Chapter Fifteen. Their opinion was that

the house could be listed at between $ 139,000 and
$ 143,000 without any repairs or improvements.

When Barry and his Mom learned of this, they
were overjoyed and listed the home with one of the
brokers at $ 139,900. The house sold in five days to a
stock broker who was going to put in about seventy-
five thousand dollars of additional money to make it
just to his wife's liking.

The real estate market reality is that you have to
be sure that the agents and brokers you deal with are
really on your side. They are out there. You just have
to be more patient and have to make them convince
you of their credentials before you list with them.

Agency Relationships- Additional Realities

Today's real estate arena has some new twists
on the way that you can deal with brokers and agents
that must be understood by you before you enter into
any monetary or legal agreements with them for the
sale of your home.

In most states, licensed real estate brokers are
considered as fiduciaries of a sort. That means that
they are in a position of "trust" (your trust) and that
they should have your best interests at the forefront.
Because most states or local boards of realtors regulate
the behavior of brokers with guidelines, statutes, rules
and regulations, a code of ethics or actual laws

and procedures, you have a certain degree of comfort level as to their honesty and integrity. But, you must be the sole judge as to whether or not they are the best agent or broker for you.

The different ways that a licensed real estate broker can relate to you in terms of their "agency" are as follows:

Seller's Agent

A seller's agent works ONLY for the seller and has legal obligations, called fiduciary duties, to the seller. These include such things as reasonable care, undivided loyalty, confidentiality, and full disclosure of facts and information relating to the sale or purchase of the seller's house.

Buyer's Agent

A buyer's agent works ONLY for the buyer. A buyer's agent has fiduciary duties to the buyer similar to the sellers agent above BUT when working with sellers agents or dual agents (those representing both parties) the buyer's agent must act honestly and may not make any mis-representations on matters material to the transaction.

Disclosed Dual Agent

A disclosed dual agent works for BOTH the

buyer and the seller. To work as a dual agent, a firm must first obtain written consent of the buyer and the seller. In other words, both the buyer and the seller must be informed that the firm has chosen to represent both buyer and seller. A good example of dual agency is when Agent A with a firm lists a house for sale and he is representing the seller as a seller's agent, and Agent B from THE SAME FIRM has a buyer who wants to purchase the house that was listed by Agent A. Both AGENT A and B are now working as dual agents in this transaction.

Transaction Broker

A transaction broker works with a buyer or a seller or both in the sales transaction without repre-senting anyone. A transaction broker does not pro-mote the interests of one party over another. A trans-action broker primarily serves as a manager of the transaction and communicates information between the parties to assist them in arriving at mutually acceptable agreement and in closing the transaction. They cannot advise or counsel either party on how to gain advantage over the other.

(Author's Note:For exact information about how the different types of agency relationships can affect you in the sale or purchase of a home, consult your real estate attorney.

FSBO— For Sale By Owner. Is it Worth It ?

Most sellers are tempted at one time or another to GO IT ALONE and try to sell their house without the assistance of a professional real estate broker.

Following are the times when this may be a good idea.

1. The market in your town is HOT. Everything is selling on your street like hot cakes. Your neighbor sold her house in one day. You can't miss.

2. You have a special type of house and have constantly gotten compliments and statements from visitors that they would love to buy it if it ever became available. It may be an historic home or a custom design or overlooking a lake with a view of a famous bridge or the city skyline. It's a one-of-a kind dream home and everyone knows it.

3. You are selling it to your kids or a family member and you know that all that has to be done is the legal and financial mechanics of the sale.

4. You have two homes and are able to live in the second while some friend, family member or employee who you trust is willing to screen potential buyers and show them the property by appointment. (See Risks section below).

5. You are a real estate broker yourself and can cut out your own commission on the sale.

Unless the above mentioned cases are yours, there appears to be many more reasons for NOT listing your home yourself:

Risks and Negatives of FSBO

1. Safety and security of your family and home.
  Who will you be letting into your house?
  Will they be "tire kickers."?
  Will they be "curious" neighbors?
  Will they be "casing" your home to rob?
  Or worse?

2. How will you know if the people you let in to see your house are financially qualified to purchase ?
  Will you see financial statements?
  Can they get a mortgage?
  Can YOU get them a mortgage?

3. Who will protect your legal rights during the home showing and home selling process?

4. You will be spending advertising dollars and will not be sure if they are in the right media.

5. You will not be in multiple listing real estate services and will not be getting maximum exposure to your intended buyer groups.

6. It is likely that you will price your house too high because of the emotional factors that make you feel that your residence is "special."

7. Real estate agents will not bring buyers to FSBO homes because it is not in their best interest to do so. They would be risking their commissions.

8. You will not know what environmental, home construction or zoning changes have occurred in your town that might have impact on the price you charge for your house or that might require you to spend unexpected funds to bring your property up to code.

9. There is no key management system. You will have to be home every time someone SAYS they are coming. Many times they will not show up.

10. You are not a marketing person and will likely decide to list with a broker after you have spent money needlessly on newspaper ads, signs, and wasted time waiting for buyers that never show up.

11. The new FSBO assistance "programs" that promise a helping hand in selling your house may not be as effective as you'd hoped. You may end up spending a lot of time and money only to find out how much you really needed a real estate professional to to an effective job in getting your house sold. Brochures and phone sales pitches can be very enticing. But unless you are a marketing person, beware this route.

Broker Referrals

A brother and two sisters were in my office one day and we were talking about their choice of a real estate broker. I was trying to explain our home marketing assistance program. I told them that it utilized experienced local brokers to establish a correct listing price on the house and then oversaw the marketing and sale process all the way through to closing.

One sister kept shaking her head (signalling no) as I spoke and repeated to me over and over that they had their broker picked out already. She didn't want to hear about anybody else. They were set. They already had the right person to get their house sold quickly and at a good price.

This didn't surprise me. It happens often as there are many excellent agents with good reputations that can get the job done quickly. Because of that reputation, they have developed followings of customers and referrals to rely upon for their supply of listings. Broker loyalty does indeed exist and is welcomed by most builders for if the agent really is good, the home will come off of contingency faster and the construction of the home will begin.

As her head continued to shake in support of "her selected agent," I yielded. "O.K.—Who is she?", I asked. She said, "I don't know her name — she's my doctor's daughter."

The doctor's daughter was a "weekend warrior" and not a full-time real estate agent. These three buyers were willing to place the responsibility of selling their house of forty-five years to a twenty-one year old who was "playing" with real estate as a hobby and as a way to earn extra money for a new car.

Please don't do that.

At your age you have likely been taking care of other people for your entire life. Children, employees, grandchildren, each other. Always looking out for the benefit of the others in your life. It's time for you to think about YOU. Be selfish. Be smart enough to know that you only have a "window of living" left and no one should get in the way of making that happen as conveniently as possible.

If you are truly seeking out a broker or agent referral, you will have to do a little work. And I know that work is O.K. with you because you've taken the steps in this book that were necessary to buy your retirement home. Keep the same enthusiasm when you're selling the old one.

Here are my recommendations for referrals of real estate agents and brokers for you to use:

— Neighbors that have recently sold or listed their houses. Go talk to them and get their recommendations.

— Family and friends that have recently listed or sold in the nearby area.

— The local Board of Realtors. Ask for a listing of the top firms by market share in your area. If they won't be specific, ask them for five recommendations of brokers to call. Or, ask for the list of their board of directors. Often these people are owners or top agents of the best firms in the county.

— The Yellow Pages (with care). The largest ads aren't always the best companies. Use the phone book to make a listing of ALL the companies. Call or write to them and see who answers in the most professional manner. You may end up with the smallest brokerage in town and the best service imaginable.

— Contact your local bank president or vice-president and ask him or her who the biggest and best brokerages are in the town. They certainly will be major depositors of the bank and the officers will not usually steer you wrong.

— Drive around and see the local brokers. Stop in the offices and see how you are treated. If they are friendly and professional in their own offices, there is a good chance that their work ethic will be evidenced in their efforts on your property as well.

— Home Marketing Assistance Companies (We will cover these in Chapter 15)

— Call the local paper's real estate editor. Tell him or her that you need to know who the biggest and the best brokers are in the area. He may refer you to past issues of the paper with specific articles on brokerages or he may just tell you who he likes best.

— Drive the area and your town and see which real estate signs are most prominent. Chances are good that if there is a lot of one company's signs, they might be one that you want to interview for your needs.

In summary, I can't emphasize enough that picking a broker is VERY important. Don't leave it to chance and don't underestimate your own ability to seek out the best one from your town that will suit your needs.

Getting the House Ready and Repairs

A few pages ago I related the story of Barry and his mother and I hope that you understood that a complete overhaul of your house may not be a prudent thing to do if you are going to sell it at a profit. In most cases, you are not likely to recover even thirty or thirty-five percent of your investment.

Certain things will have to be fixed or replaced if you KNOW that the home inspection is going to highlight them. For example, if the furnace is broken, if the roof is leaking, if the A/C hasn't worked in seven years, or if the driveway has dropped seven inches on one side. You must understand that these things will have to be addressed at some point. If your funds are low, however, and you can't afford to do these repairs yourself before the sale, you may have to make an accommodation to the buyer which is reflected as a price allowance for the work. I suggest that if this is the case with you that you "prepare" by having several quotations from local contractors for the work. That way, when your buyer's broker says that they'll deduct five thousand dollars for a new roof, you can show him three reliable quotes with the highest being $ 3700. This may save you $ 1300.

After major elements are dealt with, the essential factors to remember in an effort to "detail" your house before you put it on the market will be:

CLEANLINESS (especially kitchen and bathrooms. They must sparkle).

LACK OF CLUTTER— make sure that closets, basement, attic, and all rooms are clean and clear. You will have to have your yard sale BEFORE you sell the house.

BRIGHT AS POSSIBLE — have every light on with clean light bulbs. Have every window open and clean. Day and night — Lights on.

COSMETIC IMPROVEMENTS — you may very well have to paint interior or exterior elements of your home. Your realtor will give you suggestions in this regard. Cover worn areas of flooring with throw rugs. Replace light bulbs that are burned out or discolored. Fix the little cracks and defects that you have gotten accustomed to. It's time to get these things repaired.

Once you decide to sell your house, the first thing you will want to do is to develop a checklist of items that need to be addressed. In order to accomplish this, I suggest you do the following:

1. Observe your home as if you were a buyer. Stand across the street and really "look" at your home.

> — Is the overall appearance pleasing?
> > Landscaping neat and "alive"
> > Lawn — Green and cut
> > Shutters — straight and clean
> > Paint Job — Front door and siding
> > Trees — Do they need trimming?
> > Are the windows clean and "sparkling?"
> > Are the roof shingles attractive?
> > Is there clutter in the driveway or yard?
> > Is it clean and impressive? Really?

2. Stand at the front door, still outside your house, and make believe you are waiting for the owner to open it up and invite you in. Is the entryway inviting, clean, and a place you feel comfortable?

3. Stand in the foyer or entry area of your house. Is it also "inviting?" Is it a place that your guests feel comfortable? Does it make you feel like you want to see the rest of the house? Or make you want to leave?

4. Review each room in the house and observe how it feels to you. Is there too much furniture in it?

Are the paint and carpeting fresh and neutral colors? How will the new buyer use this room? Are the closets clear and uncluttered? Your buyers will be checking.

5. Look out the back yard and see if it is well landscaped, mowed, and uncluttered. Is the deck or patio clear and fresh? Are there any missing railings or broken fences? Does it look like the family enjoyed and USED the back yard or does it look like it has been unattended to? Spend a few dollars and freshen it up with some flower pots.

When you have completed your "review" of your own house, determine what you are able to afford to correct, what you will have to minimize, and what you will have to leave to the next owner. Understand that the more you leave for the new owner, the lower your selling price is going to be. It's a difficult situation, but most homeowners WILL survive the process.

Marketing Hint

After repairs are completed and the home is listed with a real estate broker, it will pay dividends if you will remember the key points of **CLEANLINESS, NO CLUTTER, and BRIGHTNESS**. Also, when you know a broker is bringing someone over, bake a pie, make some coffee, and leave the house for a few hours. Leave the selling to your professional broker.

PROPER REAL ESTATE BROKERAGE

In the last chapter, I mentioned that there are both good and bad real estate brokers and agents, just as there are both good and bad doctors, lawyers, storekeepers, and dry cleaners. You have to develop a skill for evaluating professionals so that you will be in control of the important aspects of your lives such as buying your retirement home or selling your house of forty years.

Good real estate brokers and agents will do many things in common while in the process of selling your house and I have listed some of them here for your review. If your agent is not acting in this way, consider a new agent.

GOOD BROKERAGE includes:

1. First listening to your needs and goals for the sale of your home. What do you need to accomplish in terms of money and timing?

2. Review of your property WITH YOU to

determine your idea of what makes your house special and (maybe) worth a little bit more to a buyer.

3. A comparative market analysis of homes sold and homes listed that REALLY are comparable to yours. (Not just a fast computer printout).

4. A formal presentation of the comparative market analysis with suggested highest price, lowest price, recommended list price, and expected sale price.

5. An explanation of the type of agency agreement that will exist between you and the broker and whether or not they will list your house in multiple listing services and cooperate with other brokers in the area.

6. A negotiated listing agreement.

7. Presentation and explanation of a marketing plan for your house that includes HOW MANY times the ads will appear in the local papers. You should get a written commitment or a schedule of advertising from the agent BEFORE you sign the listing agreement.

8. An advertising and marketing plan that includes all or some of the following:

— Multiple listing of your house
— Internet listing

— Broker's Open House date
— Public Open House date
— Mailing to your neighbors about your listing
— Attractive sign on the property
— Newspaper advertising
— Radio and cable T.V. ads
— A color brochure on your house
— Key management procedure
— By appointment only if requested
— Broker brochure mailing

9. Periodic reporting to the owner including comments from buyers that have seen the house.

10. Presentation of all offers.

11. Negotiation of all offers or contracts. Legal assistance and liaison to attorneys.

12. Mortgage assistance if required for your buyer.

13. After-sale coordination through the closing.

14. Commission disbursement to all broker entities involved in the purchase of your home.

15. Constant information resource for you on any topic of real estate pertaining to your sale.

A good broker's agent will become your friend

over the course of the sale of your home. And, if they have treated you well, it is likely that you will recommend them to friends and family when they require real estate assistance.

True real estate professionals will answer their phone calls, listen to your questions, act on your behalf, and in general gain your trust with every action that they perform. EXPECT the BEST. And don't settle for less.

HOME SELLING ASSISTANCE

For many years, there has been a small group of companies that has existed for the sole purpose of making interstate relocation of employees easier on the employee and the employer. These relocation companies range from just fee paid managers and planners of the move to real estate brokerage entities that work for commissions on the sale and purchase of the homes involved. In either case, the workload on the employee is easier and makes for a better transition to their new home.

In today's active adult marketplace, relocation companies have broadened their marketing arm to include special services for seniors who are faced with the prospect of selling a house they may have lived in for decades. In these cases, when the sellers are uncertain about how to proceed in the sale of their home, the relocation function becomes the home selling assistance service. It has been welcomed by most senior sellers who know about these companies or who are fortunate enough to be included in a builder sponsored program that is often available.

The generic home selling assistance programs in existence today generally provide the following to the senior seller:

1. Information and counsel on the local real estate market and the process of selling a home in that market.

2. Supervision of local brokers in the development of accurate comparative market analysis for the seller's house.

3. Guidance as to maximum initial listing price for most profit in the least time. (Generally, the senior market is not a patient seller.) The management company is trying to satisfy the financial needs of the seller while still accomplishing the contractual timing target as set by builder and seller (the sale of home contingency period).

4. Development of a sound marketing plan with the selected broker.

5. Supervision of the local broker's activities.

6. Continuing counsel to the sellers throughout the selling process.

7. Regular reporting of broker activity to the seller.

8. Assistance with search for interim housing and moving companies.

Many builders and developers are utilizing home selling assistance companies to make the purchase of their homes more attractive to senior buyers.

If you can imagine the typical buyer, who has been in a home for thirty or forty years, you can understand that they may need a little more "hand holding" than a buyer of thirty years of age.

When I explain the home selling assistance programs that I am familiar with I usually review what the less than professional real estate agent would do if faced with a forty year seller much as I did in the last chapter's section on market realities. I outline the worst scenario so that they will listen more intently to the program that is being offered by the builder.

When they realize that the advantages are significant in a controlled and managed home selling program, they are more likely to commit to the program and get their house sold at the best market price within the time frame they are seeking.

The builder is usually taking a building lot off of the market and reserving it for the contingent purchaser at a fixed price for a specific period of time. For that, he expects to have some control over the listing price of the house and the supervision of the listing broker that is selected.

The use of home selling assistance companies eliminates the cases where the sellers are "setting" their own prices on homes that may be ten or fifteen percent over the actual market level. It also eliminates the case where a less than caring broker lists the house "high" to get the six month listing. Then the seller is faced with one reduction after another until it is at or below market value and attracts a buyer.

Successful home selling assistance programs concentrate on four precepts that help the selling process go smoothly:

— Proactive Marketing Plan
— Proper Initial Pricing
— Professional Realtor Activity
— Personal Real Estate Management.

Proactive Marketing Plan

The seller is urged to take an active roll in the selling effort. Along with being objective in his evaluation of what has to be fixed or dressed up in the house, he may also be also asked to provide the following types of accents to help the broker sell the property:

— Make a list of local schools, colleges, shopping centers, doctors offices, hospitals, and any other sites or venues that new residents would be interested in locating.

— Take new pictures of the home in a good time of the year so that a brochure might be created by the broker for distribution to prospective buyers.

— Outline what new or renovated features of the house should be brought to the attention of visiting brokers and buyers.

— Keep the house neat as a pin during show-ings and provide some aesthetic and aromatic touches to the home environment. Baking an apple pie will fill the house with great smells. Putting out a monopoly game in the den might remind a buyer about "his" youth and make the room even more attractive.

Proper Initial Pricing

By far the most important factor in the sale of your house will be the price that it is listed at. If too high, you will not get the number of buyers necessary for a timely sale. If too low, you may sell it in a day and find that after commissions and legal fees, you don't have enough money to purchase your new home.

You must have the right balance between initial selling price and expected time on the market. For example if you price a home higher than the market price, you may have to wait six months to a year for that ONE buyer to come in that also feels that the house is worth that amount. If you have the luxury of time on your side, this is fine. But, most senior buy-ers do not want to wait six or eight months or more to find out if they are going to be able to retire to a new home. They want to know that is is going to happen soon.

Professional Realtor Activity

The management company will try and insure that the performance of the selected brokers and sales-people is maximized. They are the boss and the brokers are the employees. And you are the customer. It can work very well if the management company is good at what they do.

Incidently, good brokers usually like home selling assistance programs because they have the opportunity to get listings without going to the usual expense of solicitation or farming for leads. And, if they perform well for the management company, they may be on the list to be considered for future listings.

The home selling assistance company will be your guide throughout the selling process. And step one for them is to select the best local brokerage firms that they can find to work within the guidelines that they set up. They must be familiar with YOUR area.

Personal Real Estate Management

Senior buyers usually welcome the fact that the builder has a program to help make their home selling job easier. At the core of the process will always be the new home, or senior facility salesperson who is the real "quarterback " of the process. For it is he or she that the buyer has trusted to the point of purchasing the new home. This is just more of the same.

IT'S SOLD — NOW WHAT?

Many a couple has come into my office in shock. Almost trembling, they tell me that the house sold in two days. I can sense their elation and their confusion. It is almost overwhelming to them that the process of buying the house took them twelve months. And now, after only two days, they're going to be homeless. Oh my gosh, what now?

This case happens in both good and bad real estate markets. If the price is right and the house is a good one in a good town, it is not uncommon to see it sell in a matter of days or weeks.

The process that follows the receipt of an offer on your house will generally take on the following path all the way to closing of title. Most sellers are wary for the first few days after receiving an offer because they don't know a lot about their buyer. Who are they? Will they qualify for a mortgage? When do they want to be in? Will the lawyers be able to agree on all of the terms? Will my house hold up to the inspection process? Where will we go if we have to leave before our new home is built? Can I afford all of the closing costs on my house? What did the lawyer say he would charge for his services? These questions and others create a "blur" for a few days and no senior buyer is exempt from the anxiety of this time in their retirement process.

Typical Process After Purchase Offer Received

— RECEIVE OFFER TO PURCHASE
— Negotiations between brokers and principals
— Agreement of sale / earnest money deposit
— Attorney hired to review the contract
— Attorney review process (both sides)
— Agreement on terms of purchase
— The "dreaded" home inspection
— The buyer applies for mortgage
— Termite inspections
— Buyer mortgage pre-approval letter
— Deciding on a closing date
— Required repairs following inspection
— Negotiating other items from inspection
— Firming up the closing date
— Buyer final mortgage commitment
— Settlement sheet reviewed both sides
— Closing of title

During the period after an offer is received, sellers have to be accommodating to avoid scaring away buyers with unusual demands. For instance, they CANNOT demand that the buyer wait until their new home is finished before they can have the old house. But, they CAN ask if the buyer would be willing to "rent back" the house to them at a premium until their new home is completed. They CANNOT say that they will in no way fix a major defect that the home inspection turned up. But, they CAN offer to reduce the price of the home by a negotiated amount to account for the defect. If good judgement is used, most buyers and sellers can agree on most items without too much difficulty. For each has something the other wants. And that is a good equation.

If you are a new home purchaser, at some point in the process, usually after you are certain that a closing date has been established, you will have to decide if you are going to "start" your new home at the new community. This usually requires the payment of additionally deposit monies and the payment of a percentage payment toward ordered options. By doing so, you will be shortening the length of time that you will be "homeless" and in need of temporary housing.

Your ability to start the new home will be dependent on your financial capability and your degree of risk acceptance.

If all of your money is tied up in the old house, you may HAVE to wait until the actual closing date to get the money in hand to purchase the new one. Make sure that you ask your builder's salesperson if they will wait for you to close AFTER your contingency period has ended. Most good builders will stick by you as long as the closing date is not overly extended. Remember that this question can be brought up BEFORE you give the salesperson your reservation deposit and can also be addressed in attorney review of your purchase agreement on the new home.

When the old house is under contract and you are past attorney review and are planning closing dates, it's time to get back to your salesperson at your destination community and let him or her know what's going on. They may have some important information for you that could affect whether or not you should release your sale of home contingency. Delivery times on homes may have changed. More lots may have become available. The homeowner's association may have made some new changes to the bylaws that would affect your choice of structural options. Or prices on options might be scheduled for increases in a week and you still have time to lock in the current prices on your items of choice. Talk to them and maximize their contribution to your smooth transition.

After the house is under contract you will begin to realize and accept that your dream of a lifetime is about to become reality. Your years of work and sacrifice are going to be rewarded. You're going to get your new home and begin to enjoy your retirement in a place that you've carefully selected. A place that satisfies your needs. A new place called home. Enjoy the freedom of embarking on this new adventure.

THERE'S LAWYERS
AND THERE'S LAWYERS

As a real estate broker, I always recommend that buyers retain an attorney to review the agreement of sale to insure that their rights are being protected throughout the legal phases of the purchase. It is just good judgement on their part to do so since the new home purchase is usually over $ 100,000.

Depending on your specific experience with contracts, attorneys, and administration of legal matters that you have gained over the course of your working and personal life, you may, however, be able to guide the attorney toward your more primary concerns. This may be more cost efficient than handing him a contract and telling him to conduct a review. As with a real estate broker, the attorney also has to be aware of your needs and your finances if he is to target in on those aspects of the contract that are most important to you. Don't be afraid to tell him exactly what you are concerned about. Give him the information he needs to serve you better.

Remember too that real estate is a legal specialty. An attorney who is only familiar with wills and estate planning is not likely to be your best resource for legal guidance on the risks associated with a contract for purchase of a new home. Get a specialist. If you don't know one, ask your regular attorney for a referral. If you don't have a regular attorney, ask your banker or your accountant. But, get someone who has been referred to you or that you can get references on rather than one out of the phone book.

I usually make the following recommendations to my customers who are purchasing a home depending on their comfort level with legal instruments relating to financial matters:

Recommendation # 1

For 100% protection, retain a real estate attorney to review the agreement of sale, oversee the entire legal process through construction, and conduct the closing of title at settlement. If you are a cautious person don't read any further.

Recommendation # 2

For those with a high degree of comfort level with legal instruments and processes, read the contract yourselves and make notes of questions that you have for your attorney to address when you meet with him the first time. Retain a real estate attorney to review the contract and get you through the attorney review process successfully. Decide whether or not you will require the attorney to continue on retainer through the construction process and to conduct the closing of title. Depending on the state you are purchasing in, you may be able to use an independent title company to conduct the closing (for a fee). Or, you may be able to let the builder's closing department do the work with no fee. Your choice will depend on your confidence in the builder, the percentage of completion of the community, your micro research findings from Chapter 10 and your financial ability to afford maximum legal protection.

Recommendation # 3

If you choose not to have an attorney for review of the contract or the closing of title but rather you trust that the builder and his employees have your best interest at heart, you had better make sure through intensive investigation of existing homeowners that there has been no problems to date with the builder's reputation or with his willingness to satisfy homeowners requests throughout the course of the project.

Often, a very polished buyer will sign his agreement of sale and tell me that he's not going to use an attorney for a review of the contract. After I review the risks of not going to an attorney, he will usually reconsider and agree to discuss it with his regular attorney. That's a good start.

Doing it all yourself is risky and not recommended. But, if you insist on this non-protected way to proceed, you can be "marginally" protected so long as you know the following:

1. You must know that the builder has an exceptional, and unspoiled reputation. (Chapter 10).

2. You must have spoken to several community residents and asked them specifically if they have had any problems with their contracts, delivery times of homes, construction quality, or closing of title.

3. You must have assurances that your title insurance is being obtained by a reputable title company.

4. You must have specific conversations with your salesperson where you ask him to outline what "typical" attorney review questions usually arise. He should be able to respond to this and also add the usual resolution of the questions as well.

5. You must have a complete estimate of closing costs as part of your agreement of sale.

6. You must know what charges will be incurred by the title company for conducting the closing if the attorney is not present.

If you are considering NOT having an attorney, I urge you to reconsider at least for the review of the agreement of sale. Since you're spending over $100,000 for your home, the several hundred more that you will spend for a complete attorney review is an option that you really should consider investing in.

Usually, with the best of intentions, some attorneys will spend an inordinate amount of time and effort picking apart every sentence in a contract in an effort to provide you with a "fail-safe" agreement. This can be expensive, unrealistic, and could lead to a cancellation of your purchase whether or not it is in your best interest. Law for law's sake is not a viable goal when you are planning your next twenty years of retirement.

Please remember that this is YOUR PURCHASE — not your attorney's. If you find that your lawyer is enamored with producing pages and pages of objections and that he is inflexible beyond your expectations, consider getting another attorney.

With a good standard builder's contract of ten to twenty pages (body plus addendums), you should probably expect an attorney review letter to include from four to twelve points for negotiation or clarification. These are communicated directly to the builder's attorney and can usually be dealt with in one or two communications that are normally faxed back and forth in the course of a week to ten days.

Selecting a Lawyer

As I have said, if you don't currently have a real estate attorney you should seek a referral from your regular attorney, your accountant, or your banking officer. If you have a neighbor or friend that is a real estate attorney, that would also be a reasonable place to inquire. Try and resist going to the yellow pages for an attorney. The biggest ads may not result in the best selection.

Should the builder or your salesperson suggest local attorneys to you, you will have to interview several so that you are sure that there are no links to the builder and that he will be acting on your best behalf without any influence from the builder.

Remember that if you are selling your old house, you will need an attorney for that work FIRST. If you approach that attorney with the new agreement of sale for review, he may be inclined to do that for a very reasonable fee.

Lawyers are necessary for most of the world's legal processes. Use them wisely. And remember that while they are there to protect your interests, you are the client and YOUR opinion and instincts are important as well.

THE TRANSITION PERIOD

Now that your home is sold, you have an attorney, the contingencies of your buyer have been met, and the home and termite inspections are over, all that's left to do is go to settlement on your old house. Once you know this closing will indeed happen on a specific date, you are ready to prepare for the transition to your NEW HOME. In a few minutes we will suggest a schedule of activities for you to use to make your planning a little simpler.

Before that, the first decision you will have to make is whether or not you are going to wait until the actual settlement on the old house to start the construction of the new home. This is a financial and a risk decision. If you have sufficient funds available to move forward without going to settlement on the old residence, you can ask the builder if he will give you a closing contingency and proceed with construction AT HIS RISK pending the conclusion of your deal. This is usually not to risky for the builder and may give him advanced time to secure a building permit which can take up to a few weeks or more to obtain. If he will do this you usually risk nothing for if the closing falls through, you are not required to proceed with the purchase. If he will not grant you a closing contingency, you can still proceed relatively risk free so long as you are CONFIDENT that the closing will occur. But, you will be putting your additional deposit and any option money that you "front" in jeopardy should you fail to close.

Your other alternative, if funds are tight, is to wait for the actual closing so that you have the money "in hand" prior to starting the builder on your new home. The builder does not have a lot of patience however. And while he may wait a little while for this last transaction to conclude, he may change your pricing if it goes beyond a certain date. Remember that your contingency period expiration date will determine if he HAS TO wait for the closing to occur before forcing you to release or lose the contract price and terms and even your selected lot.

With that decision made, following is a summary activity schedule that you can follow to keep things on track:

1. Closing date on the old house set.

2. Decide to proceed with new home construction NOW or wait until the settlement on the old house occurs. If you are proceeding immediately, release your sale of home contingency, schedule the payment

of your balance of deposits due, and select your standard features and options.

Once you have released your sale of home contingency and the home is being started:

3. Make your decisions on interim housing until your new home is ready.
—Can you "rent back" your own home from your buyer?
— Can he delay occupancy until your new home is ready?
— Will you need to store your furniture?

4. Pinpoint the anticipated closing date on your new home with the builder.

5. Start to research:
— Moving companies
— Local furniture storage facilities
— Auto insurance agents
— Homeowners insurance agents
— Local banks
— Furnished interim housing locations
— Doctors
— Employment opportunities
— Local window decorating stores
— Local furniture stores
— Post office procedures at the new location
— Any other MICRO RESEARCH items at your new home location that you may need later.

6. Contract for the mover. Give approximate date. You will confirm the date after construction of the home is much further along. Most movers can use a tentative date for planning and ask you to firm it up three weeks to a month before the actual move is done.

7. Contract for furniture storage if not being done by the mover.

8. Contract for your interim furnished housing. Try for a month to month rental. But you will probably have to commit for a period of at least six months.

Closer to move-in:

9. Plan for mail delivery to new post office.

10. Address change information to friends, family and business associates.

11. Plan for utility changeovers and turn-ons at new home.
> — Phone
> — Cable
> — Gas and Electric
> — Water and Sewer

12. Confirm exact date of closing on new home and firm up date with mover.

13. Coordinate delivery of appliances, furniture,

and any other items that you are having delivered to the new home after the closing.

14. Get notice of settlement letter from builder announcing the exact date and time of closing and the amount of money to bring to settlement.

15. Coordinate with attorney and find out how much money to bring and in what form.

15. Schedule your final inspection of the home before settlement.

On Closing Day:

16. Final Inspection.

17. The closing of title.

18. Move into your new home.

The TIMELINE on the next page may be of use to you in understanding the timing of activities so that you will be clearer on which activities should be done first. You can create this kind of a schedule for your own specific situation. As soon as you know when you will release the sale of home contingency (or do your selections in the case of a non-contingent contract) you can begin to organize your activities so that everything necessary will be done in plenty of time.

SAMPLE TIMELINE TO CLOSING

CLOSE ON THE OLD HOUSE	*May 30*
Release sale of home contingency	*June 1*
Research Movers,local storage	*June 1*
Find a place to live temporarily	*June 1*
Do selections of colors and options	*June 5*
Building permit ordered	*June 6*
Actual construction begins	*July 1*
Pack up the old house	*July 10*
Move into temporary housing	*July 10*
Periodic visits to new home site	*August/Sept*
Local resident familiarization	*August/Sept*
Conclude all old house business	*August/Sept*
Inspections of the new home	*August/Sept*
New community participation	*August / Nov*
Pre-confirm expected closing date	*September*
Shop for new home furnishings	*Oct/Nov*
Measure windows for treatments	*Oct/Nov*
Local familiarization continues	*Oct/Nov*
Notice of exact settlement date	*November 10*
Confirm date and time with lawyer	*November 11*
Confirm financial arrangements	*November 11*
Transfer utilities to your name	*November 15*
Final inspection of the home	*November 18*
Closing Day - (Congratulations)	*November 19*
Move into your new home	*November 20*
Phone/cable hook-ups	*November 21*
Delivery of appliances / furniture	*November 21*
Go out to dinner with new friends	*November 22*
Seemingly endless unpacking	*November 23*

MOVING CONSIDERATIONS

Since most of you have not moved in a very long time, you may not remember that planning is more important than the actual event. If you take a lot of care in getting ready for the "big day", you will be rewarded with a smooth and easy transfer to your new home.

Before relating my suggestions to you regarding moving preparations, I want to touch on an important buying decision factor that is worth serious consideration.

Very often, a couple that is ready to buy will be in my office and I will begin to outline completely the contingent selling contract procedures that will occur. (Remember, in a contingent contract of sale, we are trying to prevent the case where the buyer has TWO homes at the same time.) When I mention that we will not start the new home until the old one is sold, the wife usually speaks up and says, "Wait a minute! Where will we live in the meantime? I'm not going to move twice! — There has to be a better way."

Understandably, she has concerns about how they will select and move into temporary housing, whether or not it will be furnished, what they will do with their own furniture in the meantime, and how they will be able to afford the whole arrangement.

The decision to buy on a contingent or non-contingent basis usually has its grounding in the financial ability of the couple and their creditworthiness to qualify for a mortgage. If they are affluent or can easily qualify for a mortgage for the new home, they may be able to afford the "luxury" of a non-contingent purchase where they set the day of closing on the new home IRRESPECTIVE of whether or not the old house is sold. Here they will most likely only have to move ONCE since they will have more control over when they put their house up for sale and when they schedule the new owner's closing and occupancy.

On the other hand, if they have a fear of having two homes at once, or if they are not capable of qualifying for a second home or mortgage, they may decide that the contingent contract is best for them. Here though, they may run the risk of having to move out of the old place into temporary housing first before the new one is finished and ready for occupancy.

Moving once or moving twice, the same careful planning will be required. The double move, however, can be disconcerting as many feel that they are "living out of a suitcase" for a one to five month period.

My philosophy on whether you should opt for non-contingent with a mortgage contingency or straight sale of home contingent contracts changes with the strength of the real estate market but in general I recommend the following:

If you don't have a mortgage on your existing house, the real estate market is sound, your home is very saleable, you're in a quality neighborhood, and there is not a high degree of competition on your street, you should investigate qualifying for a mortgage and going with a non-contingent contract. It will allow you to set the closing date on your new home as far out as you want and will give you more latitude as to when you list your house and how you price it in the marketplace. As you draw nearer to the date of completion on the new home, you can adjust the sale price on your house if necessary to sell it before you close on the new one. Or, you can just execute the mortgage, buy the new home, and pay the mortgage payments until the old house sells. Then you can pay off the mortgage, usually without any pre-payment penalty. It's a good way to go if you can.

If you are not going the non-contingent way and want the comfort of knowing that you will not have two houses at once or worse two mortgages at once, you should buy contingent on the sale of the house. If you decide to go this way, remember to ask your salesperson the important questions that follow:

1. If my old house sells and I have a closing date scheduled, is there a way you can start building my new home without risk to me?

2. If my house sells and the closing date is extended beyond the expiration of my sale of home contingency, will I be in jeopardy of having my home price raised or my lot taken away?

3. Do you have any temporary housing ideas that we might utilize?

4. If the house delivery is late, will you cover my living and storage expenses?

5. Can you recommend a local mover if I decide to move my furniture into local storage?

6. Can you recommend a local storage facility which is climate controlled?

7. Is there a local realtor that specializes in temporary furnished rentals in the area?

Most couples will try and find temporary housing near to where the new home is being built. This allows them to become more familiar with the surrounding area and also lets them "check " on the home progress while it is under construction.

Temporary housing can be fun as long as you

have the right attitude. With planning, you can make it a positive experience that passes quickly. But you have to be organized.

In a regular move from your old house to a new one, the procedure usually occurs on the same day. The movers arrive early, pack the truck, and leave for the new location. After some house cleaning, you usually follow and arrive before the movers get there— (sometimes WAY before.)

A move to temporary housing is a bit more difficult. There are a lot more things to consider and a lot more coordination of events necessary.

— You have to secure a month to month rental.
— You have to decide where you will store your furniture. (With the moving company or into local storage facility near your new home.)
— You must determine what you will "pack" for use in your temporary residence.
— You have to decide if you will make a lot of small trips to storage or if you will do it all in one trip.
— You have to coordinate the closing of the old house with the start of your temporary lease.
— You have to arrange for phone, utility, and post office service.
— You have to remember where everything is packed in the storage facility in case you need it before you move.
— You have to coordinate your lease termina-

tion with the expected date of occupancy in your new home so you won't be paying for extra months or weeks of storage or housing after your home is ready.

— You have to coordinate the move out of storage into the new home. Or choose to do it yourself.

— WOW. How on earth will you keep it all straight?

It sounds awful, and I guess it could be UNLESS you work carefully on your planning to get it organized right the first time. I think that you will be able to get it done if you look at it like a PROJECT.

The following suggestions apply to your move to the new house or the move to temporary housing. I want you to be careful and ever wary of your health and your pocketbook in all of your activities. Think about all of these items before you begin to plan. And for goodness sake, don't be embarrassed to ask for help from family and friends if needed. I'll bet there are a lot of people that want to see you move successfully. Give them a chance to show you how they really feel about you.

Before the Move

— Buy scissors, strong packaging tape and dispenser, file transfer boxes for important items, packing boxes that will not be too heavy to carry when filled, colored magic markers, and large white labels.

— Have a large yard sale. Sell what you can

and give away what you can't. Don't forget that donations to churches and charities can be tax deductions. Consult your accountant. If you need help organizing the event, talk to neighbors that have had sales or consider having a local "for profit" yard sale person organize it for you.

— Ask the kids to pick up their stuff. If they don't arrive to get their items in the basement or attic, call the Salvation Army and give it all away.

— Pack up you valuables and family memory items first. Pictures, photo albums, heirlooms, etc. Put them in specially marked boxes and keep them in your bedroom stacked against one of the walls. That will all be moved by you later in your car. You will make sure that you always know where these things are.

— Maintain a numbered BOX CONTENT register. Keep it on a clipboard that is always kept in the kitchen in a secure place. Every box you seal will be assigned a number. Box 1— photo albums— Box 2— silverware, etc. Later, you will write down which box numbers apply to which rooms in the new home. It will be your reference for unpacking once you are moved in.

— Use your garage for "staging" your boxes. Keep the cars in the driveway or on the street. The garage makes a great "organizer" of your house contents. And the movers will love it as well.

— Pack a first night "survival box". Assume that you have lost all of your household possessions. Pack what you will need to survive one night on the road. Fresh clothing, toothpaste and soap, food, drinks, extra shoes, alarm clock, matches, twenty dollars, a flashlight, extras car keys and a screwdriver. Also paper cups, plates, towels, instant coffee, extra pairs of glasses, cellular phone, a can of sterno, medicines and prescriptions etc. Have fun making up your own survival kit based on what you know about your needs.

— Pack your breakable items in specially marked boxes. Different colors if possible. Glasses, dishes, vases, should be wrapped with care. And don't make them heavy. Heavy things can be dropped.

— Pack the food items and utensils in the kitchen that are worthwhile. Give away or throw away what is not. This is your opportunity to get rid of the things that you never use. Don't bring items that will take up space in the new "smaller" home unless they are used every day or on very special occasions.

— Keep cleaning supplies packed separately and mark the boxes for easy retrieval. You will likely be looking for cleaning products soon after you move in. Don't bring anything flammable unless you can keep your eye on it constantly.

— Pack your existing luggage. Don't transport luggage or suitcases that are empty. They represent a great way to transport all of your clothing.

— Pack winter wear or infrequently used items in specially marked boxes that are destined for the attic of your new house.

— Wrap pictures and wall hanging products in bubble pack. Tape them for transport. Take the extra time to spackle the empty nail holes before you go.

Moving Day and Moving Day Concerns

— **DON'T OVER EXERT**. You're not twenty anymore. Follow your plan and don't get stressed.

— Get recommendations on moving companies before you hire them. Get references and CALL them.

— Get written proposals and make sure they have adequate insurance coverage if they lose or break something.

— Let the moving company pack for you. Do your valuables and family heirlooms yourself. But let the professionals do the rest. The extra money you spend will save you a lot of aggravation.

— See if your moving company will be able to keep your furniture in storage ON THE TRAILER. If they have adequate vans and storage facilities this may save your furniture a double move from truck to warehouse to truck. It may eliminate damaged goods.

— Consider moving your furniture into local storage facilities and then a local mover from storage into your new home. Make sure you get a recommendation on a local mover from the builder at your community. Many of your new neighbors probably had to use movers so find out who is the best in town.

— Try to schedule your move THE DAY AFTER your closing. You are usually very wound up on the day you close on your home. If you can give yourself the "breather" of one or two days, it may be beneficial to your health and even your attitude about the work and unpacking that has to be done after you get in.

— Use the kids to move boxes into the new place after you move in. Why not store some of your stuff at the kids house. They can bring it to you when you are ready for it.

— Make sure you see the movers leave your old house and make sure you are there when they arrive at your new home. You must be the orchestrator of the move. Tell them where everything goes in the new home as they move it into the residence. They will appreciate your professional attitude and organization.

— Don't tip the movers until after they unload the furniture at the new location. Say "SEE YOU LATER" when they leave, then greet them later when they arrive. Tip them if you choose to but only after every piece of furniture is in place and after all of the packing materials have been removed and placed on the truck.

— Make sure they have printed directions to the new home. You don't want them getting lost on you.

After You're In

— Once you are moved in and all of the boxes are inside, go out and get something to eat. If it is late, wait until the next morning to get to the unpacking. Your first night there should be spent in recharging your batteries, not over exerting.

— Take your time in getting settled. It doesn't matter if it takes two weeks to get organized. You have to think of your health FIRST. Go slow.

    — Don't get TOO much help too early. Tell the kids you need a few days or a week to get organized. Sometimes the help they are trying to give becomes UNBEARABLE. Don't hurt their feelings, but don't add to your aggravation.

    — Don't worry about making the window treatments perfect right away. Put a sheet or a blanket or shades on the first night. When you get the chance to get them finished — that's fine. If you thought of getting the windows measured while the house was under construction and ordered window treatments in advance of your move, they may be able to install them the day after you arrive. Many buyers have done this and it works pretty well.

    — Get you appliances hooked up first and shop for a few days worth of living. Don't confuse your move with a lot of new items to put away.

    — Introduce yourselves to the next door neighbors. If they offer to help getting a box or two out of the car, accept it. You are all in this retirement mode together and every one of your new neighbors wants to lend a hand. Don't be a hero lifting the T.V. out of the trunk of your car by yourself. Ask a neighbor for assistance.

    — Ask for any assistance that you need from the new home sales office personnel. Your salesperson will do everything he or she can to make your move-in smooth. Make your phone calls to the phone and cable companies from there as well.

    — If you need to find out where the best hardware store is or the nearest lumber yard, ask your salesperson first before going to the yellow pages. It will probably save you a few dollars.

— Don't be in a rush to put up shelves or wallpaper. Give the new home a chance to settle and make sure that nail pops are not occurring. A well constructed home with good materials will not settle or create nail pops to interfere with your interior design. But give the home a few months anyway before putting expensive and hard to install mylar wallpaper in the bathrooms. Also, give yourself a chance to "really" decide how you want your home to look.

— Don't work the whole day on your unpacking. Take the mornings to do your work and then take a half-day trip somewhere else where you can relax. If you overdo it in the first several weeks, you may end up paying for it with health problems for months after that. Be smart with your exertion. Be smart with your health.

— If there are workmen or service personnel that can assist you with routine household set-up, consider paying them to assist you.

— Consider having a cleaning service (perhaps the one the builder uses) clean your home after your first full week of occupancy. You've been very busy getting set up. This one little treat — just to get you back on track with your cleaning routine may be very helpful in reducing your stress level.

After the move, MOST OF ALL, be patient, be careful, and don't over exert in your new home.

SOCIALIZING IN YOUR NEW HOME

The process of socialization in your new home probably began over a year before you actually moved in. If you spent the amount of time that I think you did in the sales office and model center of your new community, I'll bet that you met community residents during the course of your investigation and have already made an acquaintance or two in that process.

Most communities with an active homeowner's association will welcome contract buyers into their clubhouse before they actually close on their new home. While certain events may be restricted to those "living at" the community, other functions may have open reservation policies that will allow you to attend for the same fees as the residents providing there is adequate space or seating available.

The process of interacting with your new neighbors is about the same for married couples as it is for singles in active adult communities. Exceptions do exist, however, and there can be a "grouping" after move-in by married couples on one side and singles on the other. If the social committee is aware of this natural "split" of activity groups they should try to encourage as many events as possible for both types of resident to enjoy. In most communities, with average occupancy rates of 1.8 persons per household, the acceptance of singles is just another part of life and couples may be inclined to try to "match you up" with single friends rather than to leave you out of the "couples" oriented activities such as dances and dinner parties.

Single or married or just rooming together, the following are some proven suggestions for adapting to your new environment BEFORE you move in or while your home is under construction:

1. Get the latest copy of the resident's monthly newsletter from your salesperson.
2. Review the upcoming trips or activities that are of interest to you.
— Bus trips to local attractions
— Dinner or theatre trips
— Shopping excursions
— Boat trips
— Seminars on health and finance
— Clubhouse barbeques and parties
— Outside speaker engagements
— Club and sport activities
— Committee meetings

3. Contact the person in charge of the event and ask if it would be possible to attend. If so, make a reservation and find out if there is a charge for your attendance. Remember to bring your spouse along whenever possible.

4. Visit the clubhouse every time you come to see your home under construction. You are sure to meet new friends each time you visit.

5. Ask your salesperson to introduce you to other buyers while you are visiting the sales office or model center. They will often be there at the same time as you doing selections or just checking on the status of their homes. Perhaps you will discover that they are your future next door neighbors or that they will be moving in within days of your occupancy. It's a great chance to meet your neighbors.

6. Ask you salesperson to ask the builder to plan a special get together of new buyers. The builder will often be inclined to do this and will invite other potential buyers in to see a sampling of the community lifestyle that awaits them if they purchase there.

7. Make sure you attend all holiday parties and special events that the builder plans during the sales promotion period of the community. Open houses, barbeques, and future buyer events are great opportunities to mingle. While all of the attendees may not buy there, you may be surprised and run into a long lost friend from high school. It does happen. One thing you will learn in your new environment is that it is indeed a small world.

Socialization Outside the Community

Your new home socialization will not be restricted to INSIDE your new residence or adult community. There will be a whole new world outside of your entry gates as well.

The degree to which you participate in local community affairs, volunteering, politics, or commercial activity will be up to you. But, understand that you are retired now and you will have a lot of leisure time to devote to new avenues of interest.

The following suggestions will help you adapt to the world outside your new home and possibly will unlock new vistas in your personal growth and satisfaction. As you are now not totally dependent on "regular" income in your life, you may find that minimum wages at a part-time job may be a nice supplement to your social security and pension incomes. Local businesses are always on the lookout for honest, serious, and dependable senior employees.

1. Investigate the town's senior citizen groups. There will be at least one that frequently plans events and trips for the over 55 age group of township residents.
2. Obtain the local high school and local college adult education schedules of classes. Now may be the right time for you to take up ballroom dancing or learn how to become proficient on a personal computer.

3. Purchase and read the local newspapers everyday. Don't lose touch with the activities of the all-age world, especially in your new home town.

4. Visit the local hospitals, churches, nursing homes, and assisted care living facilities. If you are in good health and can work as a part-time volunteer, you may find that this "controllable" responsibility in your life keeps you vital and more confident of your own identity.

5. Become active (again) in church or synagogue activities. Perhaps you have strayed from the regularity of religious participation. This is your chance to reevaluate your needs and become more active again.

6. Investigate part-time work in the fifteen minute driving radius of your home. You may find something just right for you.

7. Ask your salesperson if the builder has any part-time employment needs at the community during the selling process. The use of residents as hosts and hostesses in model homes has become a popular activity and a profitable one for the retired workers.

8. Plan to become knowledgeable about local politics as it relates to you and your home. Attend public open forum meetings on taxes, development, transportation issues, roads, recreation, and school issues. If you have a vote in the town's issues — USE IT. The power of the over 55 voter is very strong today. But you must show up and vote your opinions.

9. Visit and use local stores and services before you move in. Tell the store owners who you are and

that you are moving into a new community in town. Ask if they have any suggestions for you about local activities that might be of interest.

10. Visit the local library as often as you can. The employees there are often at the hub of social and commercial events in the town. Librarians also love to talk about their home towns. They can be a valuable resource for you in becoming familiar with the surrounding towns and histories.

11. Consider turning your hobby into a part-time business. Review you abilities and see if the products or services you can provide might be of use to others in your community or your town.

For example, do you:
- Make excellent crafts
- Enjoy home carpentry
- Love to decorate home interiors
- Love to clean homes
- Like to detail or decorate automobiles
- Like to decorate cakes
- Have a machine shop
- Work on decorative wood figures
- Paint or sculpt
- Love to paint houses
- Play the piano
- Like to take care of small children
- Make great fishing lures
- Love graphics or communication
- Excel at the computer
- Love to entertain
- Cook like a professional

— Enjoy framing pictures
— Love to take pictures
— Write poetry or fiction

The list goes on and on. Maybe it's time to write that book and start doing seminars across the county to share your gift with others. It's all up to you. But, I can promise you, if you do something well, you will be able to sell it or donate it to others and achieve great satisfaction in the process. So explore— investigate— and trust in your ability to produce a quality item for someone else's benefit or pleasure.

As a summary to this chapter, it can be said that each of us requires a different degree of interaction with others to be happy. But, since you have made the choice of entering into a community filled with others of common age and interests, it would appear to be a waste not to open up a little and engage in all the activities that surround you until you find the ones that are especially pleasing to you and your spouse.

In the "all-age" residential communities that most of you have left, it wasn't unusual for you to speak only to the two neighbors on either side of you for your entire time there. In your new setting, you will likely decide to increase the size of your social circle. Your pace and your process is up to you. But, in order to maximize your happiness in your new home, I suggest you keep an open mind and "assume" that your new neighbors are just as nice as you and just as nervous about life in the new community as you are.

If you investigate the steps above and do your best to BE YOURSELVES, I'm sure you'll end up with many new friends and perhaps a new part-time career.

WHAT WOULD I HAVE
DONE DIFFERENTLY?

This last chapter of my purchasing guide should not be required if you have been careful, complete, diligent, and organized in your search for and purchase of your new home or retirement residence. I am confident that you have done well and I am hopeful that I have made your decision process easier and more reliable.

The following comments are REAL. These are afterthoughts of actual buyers that I have known over the past years that have purchased in active adult communities and then had better HINDSIGHT than FORESIGHT. We all know how that works. If you think about each of these "regrets" BEFORE you make your decision, maybe the list in my next book will be shorter.

If you remember the eighteen decision factors as they relate to your physical, financial, psychological, and emotional needs, you will see that each of the following regrets could have been avoided with a little more communication or planning prior to the decision:

1. We should have realized that with our family so close to us, we would have been better off with the larger size screened porch.

2. We didn't know that the cement patio didn't have footings under it. When we tried to construct a screened porch after we moved in, we discovered that we had to break the patio up and have footings poured.

3. We should have spent the extra money and gotten a larger lot with a better view of the open space.

4. We should have asked the builder if the town was going to supply the garbage cans and found out what size they were. We didn't have a place to put them except in the garage.

5. We never should have moved our furniture into a local storage facility. The mover scratched up my mother's dining room set and we had no insurance to cover the damage.

6. I wish we had known that the movers could have kept our furniture ON THE TRAILER while our home was built.

7. We should have measured the master bedroom set BEFORE we moved in. We ended up having to trim the window sills in the new home.

8. We found out later that the builder was offering more money as an incentive than we got. We should have asked the salesperson for the best deal possible before we signed.

9. We should have visited the township offices before we bought and gotten the exact tax information

from them.

10. We should have checked out employment opportunities before we moved in.

11. We should have spent the extra money on the hot water baseboard heat. We had it in our last house and loved it.

12. We should have had our mail forwarded to the local post office for our PICK-UP a month earlier instead of waiting until we moved in.

13. We should have listened to our salesperson and taken out a forty-thousand dollar mortgage. It would have allowed us to get those extra options that we really wanted.

14. We shouldn't have played around with the electrical system after we moved in. We messed it all up and violated our builder's warrantee.

15. We shouldn't have moved on the same day we closed. It was very hectic and we felt the stress for weeks.

16. We should have had the movers pack up everything. It took us forever.

17. We should have waited to put up the wallpaper until the house settled. We ended up with cracks in the paper and had to rip it off.

18. We had window treatments measured in the builder's model instead of our actual home. The dimensions were two inches off and nothing fit right.

19. We should have put ceiling fans in every room to conserve on the air conditioning electric.

20. We should have attended more clubhouse events before we moved in. We've met so many nice

people this first week. We would have known many more if we started earlier.

21. We should have discussed where Mom would live before we selected our home model.

22. We should have taken Jared's advice and looked everywhere before we bought.

23. We shouldn't have fixed up our old house to perfection. We spent a lot of money that we didn't recover in the sale price.

24. We should have sold when the market was better. We left too much money on the table.

25. We should have bought this house two years ago when prices were lower.

26. I should have asked the exact detail of what the maintenance fees covered.

27. We should have carefully read and UNDER-STOOD the restrictions and regulations of the community before we bought.

28. We didn't know that an alarm system couldn't be easily added after the move-in.

29. We've got three pets and only two are allowed. What are we supposed to do now?

30. We should have found out exactly what the common area in the community was before we selected a lot bordering open space.

31. We shouldn't have felt that we could add a sunroom later cheaper than the builder could during construction. Our's cost us a fortune.

32. We should have investigated motor home storage sooner. We just found a place for $30 per month. But, we already got rid of our motor home.

33. We should have asked about grab bars in the master bathroom shower. We didn't need them then but we do now.

34. We underestimated the importance of the final inspection prior to closing. If we had just documented the crack in the driveway then, we would have been on record with our objection and it would have been fixed at the builder's cost, not ours.

35. We should have asked about look alike ordinances in the town. We ended up having a home of the exact same color next door to us. Neither of us thought to ask.

36. After we saw the house going up, we noticed that the ground elevation was lower than our neighbors and there was a retaining wall on our property. It would have been nice to know that sooner. We're now concerned about possible drainage problems.

37. We just found out that the perimiter community fence is on OUR property. If something goes wrong with that later, are we responsible to repair or replace it or is the Homeowner's Association?

38. When we saw the artist's rendering of the open space area, it clearly showed trees in the open area between our houses. In reality, all the trees have been taken down.

Well that's a sampling for you to consider. It by no means includes all of the comments that have been heard but it is indicative of the need for you to be careful in your investigation prior to purchase. Through careful research and after a lot of question asking, you may not have to add in your own "regrets" later.

Before we conclude our section on looking back, I want to spend a few minutes speaking to you about a question that usually comes up during the Agreement of Sale phase of the purchase of your new home. I have saved it for last because I didn't want you to start thinking about the subject too deeply until we were done with the formal presentation of our guide.

Usually, just before the checkbooks come out to give the second deposit at time of contract signing, the husband or individual buyer will say to me, "What happens if something happens to me after the contract is signed or while the home is being constructed?" "What if one of us dies or gets into a serious health condition that precludes our moving foreword with the closing?"

I have been fortunate and have only worked at developments where the builder has been sympathetic to this question and has been able to convince the buyer that they will do the right thing to resolve the matter fairly. But, since the question is so important, I want you to ask your salesperson what their builder would do BEFORE you give them your deposit money. The options available are as follows:

1. In the worse case scenario, the builder may

hold you accountable for the full home purchase, legally force you to close title and sue you for the full price of the home if you resist. Your only avenue of recourse would be to put the house up for sale on the resale market after you closed title and hopefully sell it at near the price you paid.

2. The builder (most good builders) would hold your deposit monies and put the house back on the market at the sales office and try to sell it to another prospect. Upon the closing of title, you would receive your deposit monies back and all or a portion of your option monies that had been prepaid after deducting any extraneous legal or sales costs that had been incurred in the process.

3. The builder might refund your entire deposit and prepaid option monies immediately and continue with the house as a speculation home for sale to others. This usually would only occur if sales were very strong and the project was near completion.

If you have serious concerns about this important issue, you might consider bringing this up with your attorney at the attorney review step of your contract process. You may be able to insert wording that will alleviate your fears entirely.

Regarding the couple's decision to proceed or not proceed with the purchase or construction of the home after a spouse's death or major health event, it has been my experience that the couple that has spent upwards of twelve months planning their purchase of a retirement home in a new community will likely continue on with the decision to move even after something occurs to one of the spouses. Likewise, after a couple moves into the new home, the remaining spouse after a sudden and untimely death is likely to STAY there because it was the last major decision the couple made together before the unfortunate departure. Reinforcing that decision, there is undoubtedly a sizeable new "support group" at the new adult community where death is dealt with on a more frequent level.

Well, that's it folks.

For now, my task is completed. Yours may just be beginning.

In Part I of this guide, I've tried to prepare you with a process for making a sound decision about the selection of your new home. I've outlined the important activity steps needed BEFORE YOUR DECISION TO PURCHASE. From establishing your needs to the placement of your reservation deposit, you may spend 12 to 18 months gathering information, communicating your feelings, and investigating the most important factors in your decision. This is important time for you and it should be spent wisely if you are to be happy in your new location.

In Part II of this guide, I've touched on some of the processes and paperwork that you'll have to become familiar with during the purchasing and legal procedure. Remember that your salesperson is your first line of information on the purchase of your home. Rely on him or her every time you have a question.

The next step is yours. Your choices are as follows:

1. Put this book on the shelf or give it to a friend and stay right where you are. You don't have to move, remember. That's always your first choice. And it may be the right answer for you. But, if you do decide to stay where you are, don't punish yourselves by visiting all of the shiny new communities that keep popping up around you. Be content where you are and make the best of it.

2. Take your spouse or a friend to a few active adult communities, retirement residences or assisted living campuses and get a feel for what is being offered. Talk to the kids about the changes you are considering and tell them that SOMETHING is going to happen. Then go to choice three below.

3. Go back to Chapter One and get started today on the process of selecting your retirement home and location. If you do that, it is likely that 12 to 18 months from today you will be moving into a retirement residence or your new dream home in the com-

munity of your choice. Remember, you'll be just at the beginning of the next "blessed" window of your lives.

I want to hear from you.
You may forward questions or comments to me at my E-Mail Address as follows:

JAREDMARCH@MSN.COM

I wish you the very best that life has to offer.

Jared March

Our Old House — Our New Home

BOOK ORDER FORM

PLEASE SEND ME _____ ADDITIONAL COPIES OF OUR OLD HOUSE—OUR NEW HOME (12.95RETAIL) PLUS TAX, FIRST CLASS POSTAGE AND HANDLING PER THE FOLLOWING PRICE SCHEDULE.

FOR 1 BOOK SEND $ 14.95 TOTAL

FOR 2 BOOKS SEND $ 27.95 TOTAL

FOR 3 BOOKS SEND $ 38.95 TOTAL

FOR 10 OR MORE BOOKS -----$ 11.95 EACH
(we pay postage)

____BOOKS @ 11.95 = _$_____ENCLOSED

**My check is enclosed PAYABLE to:
Jared March Publishing Group
714 West Bay Avenue
Barnegat, NJ 08005**

**Credit Card Orders:
Call 609-660-2200**

(Toll free in New Jersey) — 1-877-4 JARED M

(Cut out all pages and make copies)

Community Name_____

Phone Number _____

Salesperson _____ **Ext.** _____

Town/Municipality _____

I HAVE:

☐ **Price List (Last Increase_____Next Increase_____)**

☐ **Brochure and Floorplans**

☐ **List of Options**

☐ **Model As Is Options**

☐ **Public Offering Statement**

☐ **Rules and Regulations**

☐ **Standard Features List**

☐ **Real Estate Taxes per model**

☐ **Utility Estimates**

☐ **Preliminary Lot Grading Plans**

Date of Opening _____
Total # Homes_____
Number Occupied_____
Number Sold_____
Number of Phases_____
Est. Compl'n. Date____
Latest occupancy _____

Gas_____ **Company**_____

Electric_____**Company**_____

Water and Sewer_____**Company**_____

Cable_____ **Company**_____

Maintenance Fee_____

Includes: _____

I Pay for _____

UNDERSTAND THE PURCHASING PROCESS:

The Reservation Policy_____

The Sale of Home Contingencies Available_____

Home Marketing Assistance Programs Available

Mortgage Programs Available_____

MODEL I LIKED BEST:

Name_____B/R____BATH ____ S/F_____

Base Price:_____ As Shown: _____

I Have:

☐ Taken Photos_____(Inside and Outside?)

☐ Floorplans

☐ Flooring Guides

☐ Priced up Options with Salesperson:

    Options I will add to this house:

<u>Option</u>   <u>Price</u>

_____

_____

_____

MODEL I LIKED SECOND BEST:

Name_____B/R____BATH ____ S/F_____

Base Price:_____ As Shown: _____

I Have:

☐ Taken Photos_____(Inside and Outside?)

☐ Floorplans

☐ Flooring Guides

☐ Priced up Options with Salesperson:

    Options I will add to this house:

<u>Option</u>   <u>Price</u>

_____

_____

_____

Construction time to build:_____

Roof Material:_____ Siding Material_____

Sheathing material:_____Roof Material:_____

Type of 2x4 Studs Used_____

Basements_____ Crawl Spaces_____ Attics_____

Type of Slab Construction_____

Standard Heating_____

List of Standard product vendors:

     Plumbing_____

     Heating_____

     Air Conditioning_____

     Water Heater_____

     Roofing_____

     Siding_____

     Lighting_____

     Bathroom Fixtures_____

     Windows_____

     Appliances_____

Builder's name and address: _____

_____

Other communities built:_____

_____

_____

Standard Warranties: _____

_____

_____

Framing Walk Through: _____ Closing_____

Homeowners Warranty Period and Company:_____

_____

Are Spec Homes Available for immediate occupancy?____

Closing Cost Estimates:_____

Construction Changes Allowed?:_____

What's Special About This Community?_____

_____

_____

_____

Surrounding Amenities: Names, locations and mileage.

Hospital_____

Golf Courses_____

Beaches_____

Doctors Offices_____

Shopping Mall_____

Fire and Rescue_____

Police Department_____

Library_____

Emergency Medical Services_____

Homeowners Association Information:

☐ Public Offering Statement (copy or read in office)

☐ List of committees already formed

☐ Monthly Newsletter

☐ Names of Trustees

☐ Number of homes when control passes to homeowners.

Clubhouse Contents:

☐ Floorplan Available?

☐ Date to be completed?_____

☐ Special Feature I like_____

_____

Features that are Missing_____

_____

What are the biggest drawbacks of this community for me?

_____

_____

_____

_____

_____

Below are listed my most important purchasing factors.
At the right is my belief that this community will or WILL
NOT meet my needs:

	WILL	WILL NOT

Is this one of my top three community picks?_____

Dates Visited This Community:

_____

_____

_____

Ranking of this community:

Best ➤━━━━━━➤ Worst

1 2 3 4 5 6 7 8 9 10 11 12 13